The PROMATCH™ Essential FOOTBALL BOOK

Written by
Marc Goldberg

LEVINSON BOOKS

First published in Great Britain by Levinson Books Ltd in 1996

10 9 8 7 6 5 4 3 2 1

Text © Marc Goldberg 1996
Illustrations by James Griffiths © Goala Ltd 1996
Additional Illustrations by
James Magee, David Barnett, Alan Atfield, Matt Read
John Woodhouse, Ian Fraser-Jackson, Alex Weir © Goala Ltd 1996

A CIP record for this title is available from the British Library.
The author asserts the moral right to be identified as the author of the work

ISBN 1-86233-050-6

Reprographics by Graphico, Norwich
Printed and bound in Italy

Contents

Preview to the Premiership 1996/97

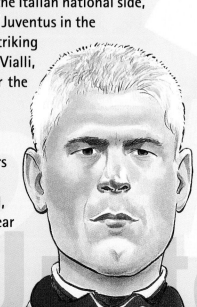

Football is taking a great leap forward this season, with the Premiership fast becoming the greatest league in the world and we, the fans, are lucky enough to be part of it. This season has seen international superstars in their prime arriving on British shores, which is a distinct improvement from past seasons when foreign arrivals were often past their best.

After last season's fantastic finale, with Manchester United taking the Premiership title once again, the race for this season's Championship does genuinely seem more evenly matched – although United's new arrivals make them a formidable force.

Newcastle looked as though they were happy to go through the summer without using their cheque book, until it was announced that they had signed Alan Shearer in a world record-breaking £15 million deal; a move which delighted Geordie fans and made Newcastle a strong contender for the title. Kevin Keegan, in seeking a winning formula, again faces selection problems. He could find himself in the same position as last season - having numerous good players but only being able to play 11 at a time.

The talking point of the summer transfer merry-go-round was the arrival of international superstars: Fabrizio Ravanelli joined Bryan Robson and Middlesbrough for £7.5 million, and has since played a significant part in improving the world-status of the Premiership; Ravanelli, at the peak of his career as a regular in the Italian national side, has moved to 'Boro after scoring for Juventus in the European Cup final. His former striking partner at Juventus, Gianluca Vialli, also came to England, opting for the bright lights of London where he joined Ruud Gullit, at Chelsea.

Chelsea may well prove to be title contenders this year, having taken on another Italian, Roberto di Matteo, and French international, Frank Leboeuf. Other stars gracing us this year are players such as Karel Poborsky and Jordi

Cruyff for Manchester United, Florin Raducioiu and Paulo Futre for the rejuvenated West Ham, Patrik Berger for Liverpool and Aljosa Asanovic for Derby – to name a few!

Possibly, the arrival of international talent has jeopardised the talent and tradition of the English League, but the transfer activity involving British players has also been very busy – Gary McAllister moved to Coventry in a shock £3 million move, and Lee Sharpe has gone to rivals Leeds, for £4.5 million. In fact, every club has bought new players in a frenzy of transfer activity.

There are signs that managerial casualties will grow as the season progresses, yet one man unfazed by this is Graeme Souness, who's returned from a spell in Turkey to manage Southampton. While international supremo Arsene Wenger has taken over from Bruce Rioch at Arsenal, the most exciting new manager to watch is Ruud Gullit; after watching him assess matches for television during the European Championships his ideas seem brilliant – but can he put them into practice?

Exciting times lie ahead for the three promoted clubs: Sunderland, Derby and Leicester. All three have struggled to gain access into the top flight, so they will fight to secure their Premiership positions.

So, with another exciting season upon us, the aspirations of fans all over the country wait to be fulfilled. Who will take the title this year? Just another few months to find out!!!

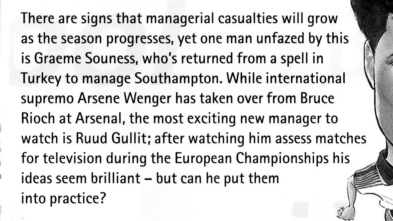

Preview to the Premiership

David Seaman
Goalkeeper

Place of Birth   Rotherham, England
Height   1.93m
Date of Birth   19-09-63
Weight   93kg

David Platt
Midfielder

Place of Birth   Chadderton, England
Height   1.78m
Date of Birth   10-06-66
Weight   77kg

David may be the world's most expensive player, having clocked up over £22 million in transfer fees, but that does not stop him getting bogged down by injuries. The 95-96 season was a non-starter for David, as he had to have two knee operations which kept him out of both his club and country sides.

The 96/97 season looks likely to be the turning point for David, as he has finally obtained full fitness and is looking forward to returning to the Highbury midfield, where he can boss the centre of the park and make the runs which made him such a desired star.

The ex-Rotherham and QPR goalkeeper has at last proved himself to be the undisputed England No.1, and many also claim that he is the best keeper in Europe.

His exploits in Euro 96 proved his ability as a great shot-stopper, a superb cross-handler and a brilliant penalty-saver, as he guided England to the semi-finals. David admits that England caps are a bonus, but the most important thing is keeping clean sheets for Arsenal. It was these clean sheets towards the end of last season that earned Arsenal a spot in the 1996 UEFA Cup.

Tony Adams
Defender

Place of Birth   London,
                 England
Height   1.86m
Date of Birth   10-10-66
Weight   87kg

Life at Arsenal would seem very different without their inspirational skipper. However, the team has had to get used to just that as the centre-half has been dealt one injury blow after another for much of 1996.

Tony managed to make a comeback to spearhead England's Euro challenge, but once again suffered a pre-season setback to the 96-97 campaign. Fortunately, Arsenal have strength in abundance to cover that position, but every player knows that Tony's full recovery will lead to an instant position in the team. Arsenal's new manager, Arsene Wenger, is sure to take full advantage of Tony's passion, desire and reliability; he is a true professional. And after his dignified admission of alcohol problems, no one can doubt his strength of character.

Paul Merson
Striker

Place of Birth	London, England
Height	1.83m
Date of Birth	20-3-68
Weight	78kg

So many people considered the Merse a spent force after his open admission of drink, drugs and gambling addictions, that it would not have been surprising if he had decided to quit football. However, Paul is a much stronger character than that and his aim was to regain his first team place.

He did this in the best possible fashion, and many of the Highbury faithful voted him their player of 95-96. This signalled a miraculous return, and Glenn Hoddle completed Paul's rehabilitation by rewarding him with an international call-up.

Ian Wright
Striker

Place of Birth	Woolwich, England
Height	1.75m
Date of Birth	03-11-63
Weight	73kg

This colourful character's Arsenal career seemed to have been in jeopardy towards the end of last season with major conflict between Ian and former manager, Bruce Rioch.

Although it was a troubled season at Highbury for 'Wrighty' he still finished top scorer with 15 Premiership goals and eventually formed an exciting partnership with Dennis Bergkamp.

He started the new season surrounded by controversy, having voiced his opinion about his troubles in his autobiography. Ian will now have to win the fans over once again!

Dennis Bergkamp
Striker

Place of Birth	Amsterdam, The Netherlands
Height	1.83m
Date of Birth	18-05-69
Weight	78kg

Deadly Dennis, the £7.5 million striker, has now become a firm favourite with the Highbury crowd. After a sluggish start to his Highbury career, he is now one of the first on the team sheet. The former Ajax and Inter Milan forward arrived at Arsenal to mixed reviews, but it seems that his career is starting to fulfill the potential it has always hinted at. With recent managerial changes, Dennis now knows that his place is secure and hopes to be a regular scorer for the Gunners this season.

STATS AND FACTS

Manager: Arsene Wenger

Captain: Tony Adams

Colours: Home - Red and White

Away - Navy and Teal

Ground: Highbury

TITLE ODDS

16/1

ON AUGUST 17th, START OF SEASON

CLUB HONOURS

LEAGUE
Champions:
1930-31, 1932-33,
1933-34, 1934-35,
1937-38,1947–48,
1952–53, 1970–71,
1988–89,1990–91

FA CUP
Winners:
1930, 1936, 1950,
1971, 1979, 1993

LEAGUE CUP
Winners: 1987, 1993

EUROPEAN CUP WINNERS' CUP
Winners: 1994

What are their chances?

With all the trouble that has surrounded the Gunners during the pre-season, it seems that they are now trying to put it all behind them and let their football do the talking. New man Arsene Wenger's experience and ideas should bring a whole new era to Highbury, where flair and excitement have been missing for years.

New signing, Vieira, has a talent that will delight the crowd and if players in the class of Seaman, Adams and Bergkamp can gel, a title push is certainly in reach.

INS AND OUTS

INS	OUTS
John Lukic **Leeds**	Mark Flatts
Patrick Vieira **Milan**	
Remi Garde **Strasbourg**	

INTERNATIONAL PLAYERS

David Seaman
England

•

Tony Adams
England

•

Dennis Bergkamp
Holland

•

John Hartson
Wales

•

Glenn Helder
Holland

(below)

SEAMAN 1

DIXON 2 **ADAMS** 6 **KEOWN** 14 **WINTERBURN** 3

VIEIRA 4

PLATT 7 **PARLOUR** 15

MERSON 9

BERGKAMP 10 **WRIGHT** 8

TEAM POSITIONS AND LINE-UP

1	David Seaman (GK)	17	David Hillier
2	Lee Dixon	18	Steve Morrow
3	Nigel Winterburn	19	Remi Garde
4	Patrick Vieira	20	Chris Kiwomya
5	Steve Bould	21	Eddie McGoldrick
6	Tony Adams	22	Ian Selley
7	David Platt	23	Paul Dickov
8	Ian Wright	24	John Lukic (GK)
9	Paul Merson	25	Scott Marshall
10	Dennis Bergkamp	26	Lee Harper
11	Glenn Helder	27	Paul Shaw
12	Andy Linighan	28	Stephen Hughes
13	Vince Bartram (GK)	29	Adrian Clarke
14	Martin Keown	30	Gavin McGowan
15	Ray Parlour	31	Matthew Rose
16	John Hartson		

Gareth Southgate
Defender

Place of Birth	Watford, England
Height	1.83m
Date of Birth	03-09-70
Weight	80kg

Mark Bosnich
Goalkeeper

Place of Birth	Fairfield, Australia
Height	1.85m
Date of Birth	13-01-72
Weight	86kg

Some questioned Brian Little's decision to splash out £2.5m on Gareth in 1995. Now, everyone looks at the acquistion as a 'bargain-buy'. Gareth's versatility is an extremely useful asset, but he proved throughout the 95/96 campaign that his best position is at the heart of defence. His mature performances during Euro 96 where barely marred by his missed penalty in the shoot-out against Germany. It is no coincidence that Aston Villa's successful season coincided with Gareth's great form.

Terry Venables was one of the first to recognise Gareth's ability and consequently threw him in at the deep end in the European Championships by playing him in every game. Gareth responded like a true professional and his impressive start to the 96/97 campaign indicates he has put the disappointment of the 'penalty miss' behind him.

The Aussie keeper is another great prospect who may be denied the opportunity to perform on the biggest stage because of his nationality. Australia may never qualify for a major world tournament, but that will take nothing away from Mark's stature as a player.

Although he was injured at the beginning of the 1996 season, he is still without doubt Brian Little's first-choice keeper. Mark's performances in last season's Coca-Cola Cup were vital to his side's success, though Villa's early elimination from the U.E.F.A. Cup has denied him a wider audience.

Ugo Ehiogu
Defender

Place of Birth	London, England
Height	1.88m
Date of Birth	03-11-71
Weight	84kg

After an impressive past few seasons, Ugo has now firmly established himself at the heart of the Aston Villa defence where he has formed a partnership with Gareth Southgate, which has proved formidable to break down.

Although his performances were good enough to merit a place in the England squad, his experience was not sufficient to see him through to the final Euro 96 22.

Villa will rely heavily on Ugo this season, especially as they're desperate to mount a title push. A solid base at the back will give the whole team confidence.

Savo Milosevic
Striker

Place of Birth	Bijelina, Bosnia
Height	1.85m
Date of Birth	02-09-73
Weight	85kg

A change in personnel up-front for Aston Villa at the start of the 95/96 campaign suggested that goals might be hard to come by – usually strikers need time to settle in at a club and get used to working with a new partner. However, the Milosevic/ Yorke partnership was an instant success and blossomed throughout the season.

Savo the Serbian is tagged as a typical 'English centre-forward', and has certainly managed to give English defences a run for their money.

Even though Savo netted a respectable number of goals last season, his running off the ball often provided him with more chances in a game than he actually managed to convert. He will be aiming to improve his goal ratio this season, and hopefully lead Aston Villa to domestic victories.

Mark Draper
Midfielder

Place of Birth	Long Eaton, England
Height	1.78m
Date of Birth	11-11-72
Weight	78kg

Mark's career in the Premiership has taken him to heady heights and his reputation is ever-increasing. After a spell at Leicester, he joined Brian Little again at Villa where his all-round game has been quite superb.

After a £3.5 million move to the 'Villans', Mark's head was in the clouds somewhat, yet his determination on the pitch is always an outstanding asset and brings confidence to his team-mates.

This season, Mark has been part of Glenn Hoddle's plans and was called up to the first squad of the World Cup qualifying campaign; this reflects how far Mark has come in the past three years.

Dwight Yorke
Striker

Place of Birth	St Clair's, West Indies
Height	1.80m
Date of Birth	03-11-71
Weight	76kg

The Trinidad and Tobago international set Villa Park alight last season with a series of dazzling performances and breathtaking goals.

Even opposition supporters find it hard to dislike Dwight, thanks to his pleasant personality and smiling face. He is a rare breed among strikers, as he is content to get his fair share of tap-ins as well as scoring a number of long-range efforts; Brian Little hopes that after a slow start, Dwight, will re-discover last season's form.

Aston Villa
STATS AND FACTS

TITLE ODDS
20/1
ON AUGUST 17th, START OF SEASON

Manager: Brian Little
Captain: Andy Townsend
Colours: Home - Claret, White and Sky Blue
Away - White and Claret
Ground: Villa Park

CLUB HONOURS

LEAGUE
Champions:
1893–94, 1895–96, 1896–97, 1898–99, 1899–1900, 1909–1910, 1980–81

FA CUP
Winners: 1887, 1895, 1897, 1905, 1913, 1920, 1957

LEAGUE CUP
Winners:
1961, 1975, 1977, 1994, 1996

EUROPEAN CUP
Winners: 1982

EUROPEAN SUPER CUP
Winners: 1983

What are their chances?

Brian Little's side was seriously underestimated last season and this year Villa are certainly good enough for a title push. With additions such as the very talented Sasa Curcic and Portuguese wing-back Fernando Nelson, the continental touch adds flair and skill to strength and solidity. Villa's side is the best they have had for years and their loyal fans are quietly confident that they can improve upon their 1996 Coca-Cola Cup win.

INS AND OUTS

INS	OUTS
Sasa Curcic **Bolton**	Paul Browne **Raith**
Fernando Nelson **Sporting Lisbon**	

① BOSNICH

④ SOUTHGATE **⑯ EHIOGU** **③ STAUNTON**

⑮ NELSON **⑭ WRIGHT**

⑧ DRAPER **⑥ TOWNSEND** **㉖ CURCIC**

⑨ MILOSEVIC **⑩ YORKE**

TEAM POSITIONS AND LINE-UP

1 Mark Bosnich (GK)	13 Michael Oakes (GK)
2 Gary Charles	14 Alan Wright
3 Steve Staunton	15 Fernando Nelson
4 Gareth Southgate	16 Ugo Ehiogu
5 Paul McGrath	17 Lee Hendry
6 Andy Townsend	18 Carl Tiler
7 Ian Taylor	19 Gareth Farrelly
8 Mark Draper	20 Riccardo Scimeca
9 Savo Milosevic	21 Franz Carr
10 Dwight Yorke	22 Phil King
11 Tommy Johnson	23 Neil Davis
12 Julian Joachim	24 Scott Murray
	26 Sasa Curcic

Tim Flowers
Goalkeeper

Place of Birth	Kenilworth, England
Height	1.90m
Date of Birth	03–02–67
Weight	90kg

After leaving Southampton to great acclaim, Tim joined Dalglish and Jack Walker at Blackburn and became the most expensive goalkeeper in contemporary British football.

Tim's goal-saving reflexes are unparalleled, yet his performance in the 95/96 season was inconsistent and this is possibly why he did not make a serious challenge to the number one jersey for England.

However, with Alan Shearer gone, Tim is next in line to be the shining star of Blackburn this year and his chirpy personality is well-suited to goalkeeping.

Graeme le Saux
Defender

Place of Birth	Jersey, Channel Islands
Height	1.78m
Date of Birth	17–10–68
Weight	77kg

Graeme had hoped to confirm his place as the number one attacking left back in the country during the 95/96 season. However, the ex-Chelsea star quickly found out that football is a very unpredictable game when a freak tumble resulted in a serious leg break.

The injury forced the Channel Islander out of Euro 96, and he has now set himself the target of returning by Christmas 1996. He will also be hoping that new England coach, Glenn Hoddle, remembers previous performances.

Colin Hendry
Defender

Place of Birth	Keith, Scotland
Height	1.85m
Date of Birth	07–12–65
Weight	79kg

Known to some as the 'white-headed warrior', Colin certainly has the winning instinct that every manager wants in a player. There can surely be no doubt that, over the past five years, the improvement in Colin's game is equal to many top players in the Premiership – including Ferdinand, Fowler and even Alan Shearer. Although Blackburn's success has often been attributed to Shearer, Alan would be the first to say that Colin Hendry's reliability, consistency and courage have been just as important.

After the recent departure of Shearer, Blackburn seem to be experiencing a transitional period, but Colin's performances still manage to shine on a weekly basis.

He showed his ability on an international scale in the European Championships against world-class strikers such as Bergkamp, Kluivert, and Turkyilmaz – all of whom failed to get passed him.

Lars Bohinen
Midfielder

Place of Birth	Vadso, Norway
Height	1.85m
Date of Birth	08-09-66
Weight	77kg

After starting his career in his home country of Norway, and then having a spell in Switzerland, he came to Britain to join Nottingham Forest. Lars became a firm favourite with the crowd but was then tempted away to Blackburn in a £1.9 million deal.

He is a player with lots of ideas, and resembles an Italian or Brazilian player rather than a Scandinavian. Lars is aiming for a successful season as he attempts to bring the good times back to Ewood Park.

Georgios Donis
Striker

Place of Birth	Frankfurt, Germany
Height	29-10-69
Date of Birth	1.80m
Weight	76kg

Blackburn's first buy of the summer was the Greek star, Donis. He is a winger with great pace, and Ray Harford hopes that he will add to Blackburn Rovers' fire-power up front.

Donis was first spotted by the British public in the Champions League for Panathinaikos where he tore defences to shreds.

He certainly appears to be a shrewd investment as his direct running could ease the pain of Shearer's departure.

Tim Sherwood
Midfielder

Place of Birth	St. Albans, England.
Height	1.85m
Date of Birth	02-02-69
Weight	80kg

Despite numerous newspaper articles speculating about Tim's future, he has firmly pledged his future to the Ewood Park club even after the departure of striking duo, Mike Newell and Alan Shearer.

Tim was the captain of the side that won the League title, and even though Kenny Dalglish has now left the club, he left behind a worthwhile legacy when he paid Norwich City for Tim's services.

Tim himself will admit that he still does not get enough goals from midfield, but Ray Harford knows that Tim's main job is to track opposition midfield runners.

Blackburn Rovers

STATS AND FACTS

Manager: Ray Harford

Captain: Colin Hendry

Colours: Home - Royal Blue and White

Away - Yellow and Navy

Ground: Ewood Park

TITLE ODDS
33/1
ON AUGUST 17th,
START OF SEASON

CLUB HONOURS

LEAGUE
Champions: 1911-12,
1913–14, 1994–95

FA CUP
Winners: 1884, 1885, 1886,
1890, 1891, 1928

INS **AND** OUTS

Georgios Donis	Alan Shearer
Panathinaikos	Newcastle
	Mike Newell
	Birmingham

What are their chances?

After the loss of stars Kenny Dalglish and Alan Shearer, it seems that Blackburn's season will either be do or die. Their team appears full of very inexperienced Premiership players who lack the confidence and cutting edge that is needed. After seasons of success and excitement, Blackburn fans might be looking at a disappointing season, with their team going through major changes.

Team formation

1 FLOWERS

2 COLEMAN 5 HENDRY

20 BERG 6 LE SAUX

22 BOHINEN 4 SHERWOOD

21 DONIS 11 WILCOX

16 SUTTON 14 FENTON

(above)
Jeff Kenna
Eire

■

Tim Flowers
England

■

Chris Coleman
Wales

■

Colin Hendry
Scotland

■

Billy McKinlay
Scotland

■

Henning Berg
Norway

■

Georgios Donis
Greece

■

Lars Bohinen
Norway

■

Graeme Le Saux
England

■

Kevin Gallagher
Scotland

INTERNATIONAL PLAYERS

TEAM POSITIONS AND LINE-UP

1	Tim Flowers (GK)	16	Chris Sutton
2	Chris Coleman	17	Billy McKinlay
3	Jeff Kenna	18	Niklas Gudmundsson
4	Tim Sherwood	19	Adam Reed
5	Colin Hendry	20	Henning Berg
6	Graeme Le Saux	21	Georgios Donis
7	Stuart Ripley	22	Lars Bohinen
8	Kevin Gallagher	23	Garry Flitcroft
11	Jason Wilcox	24	Paul Warhurst
12	Nick Marker	25	Ian Pearce
13	Shay Given (GK)	32	Damien Duff
14	Graham Fenton	33	Damien Johnson
15	Matt Holmes	34	Gary Croft

Michael Duberry
Defender

Place of Birth Enfield, England
Height   1.85m
Date of Birth   14-10-75
Weight   85kg

Some Chelsea players were fortunate enough to be guided by both Hoddle and Gullit last season, and Mike Duberry was one of the youngsters who certainly benefited from their expertise.

When Frank Sinclair and Erland Johnson suffered injuries at the start of the 95/96 season, some Chelsea fans began to complain that Hoddle did not dip into the transfer market for a replacement. But Glenn realised Mike's potential and was confident enough to throw him in at the deep end. Mike immediately fulfilled Hoddle's expectations, and quickly began to attract the attention of top clubs such as Manchester United, who recognised his potential.

Frank Leboeuf
Defender

Place of Birth Marseille, France
Height   1.84m
Date of Birth   22-01-68
Weight   76kg

Ruud Gullit's reputation means that he has no great difficulty in attracting top stars such as Di Matteo and Vialli, but in his search for a top-class centre half, he turned to the Frenchman.

Although Leboeuf is not as big a household name as Chelsea's other imports, Gullit certainly believes that he has invested in a player who is worth every penny of the £2.5 million spent on him, and who is going to argue with Gullit?

Roberto Di Matteo
Midfielder

Place of Birth Schaffhausen, Switzerland
Height   1.79m
Date of Birth   13-1-70
Weight   75kg

The baby-faced star was the surprise summer arrival at Stamford Bridge, and people doubted whether Ruud Gullit was right to fork out £4 million for a relatively unknown player.

However, Gullit knew what he was doing having watched Di Matteo's progress through the Lazio side with the passing ability that once saw Dino Zoff select him ahead of Paul Gascoigne.

Roberto is the dream midfielder, his passing is excellent, he makes up large distances in order to tackle and defend, and he also gets his fair share of goals.

He is likely to team up (brilliantly) with Vialli and Leboeuf.

Mark Hughes
Striker

Place of Birth	Wrexham, Wales
Height	1.75m
Date of Birth	01-11-63
Weight	75kg

'Sparky' has been an instant hit with the Stamford Bridge faithful since his £1.5m move from Manchester United. Glenn Hoddle initially purchased the Welshman for a number of reasons – for example his ability to hold the ball, his goals and his experience.

Mark's first full season at Chelsea proved a moderate success as his aggressive attitude provided a neat balance to Chelsea's continental style of football.

When Ruud Gullit took over as manager in the summer of 1996 he instantly recognised Chelsea's need for another striker. Some believed the acquisition of Vialli would be at the expense of 'Sparky', but instead Ruud recognised the benefits to be gained from playing the two together and the partnership has worked well.

Gianluca Vialli
Striker

Place of Birth	Cremona, Italy
Height	1.74m
Date of Birth	9-07-64
Weight	77kg

Surely one of the greatest transfer coups of all time sees the arrival of Gianluca into the Premiership.

Following a 1996 European Cup Final success with Juventus, he has arrived at Stamford Bridge to join an old friend and colleague, Ruud Gullitt.
After spending his entire career playing in allegedly the best league in the world, Serie A, he was attracted by the variety and excitement of the Premiership, not to mention the bright lights of London!

Whether or not Vialli can adapt to the English game is a major question; after playing with footballing superstars such as Roberto Baggio, Allessandro del Piero and Walter Zenga.

Dennis Wise
Midfielder

Place of Birth	Kensington, England
Height	1.68m
Date of Birth	16-12-66
Weight	63kg

The nippy midfielder has matured significantly since his early days as part of the now famous Wimbledon 'Crazy Gang'. His game has improved to such an extent that Glenn Hoddle rewarded him with the Chelsea captaincy before he left for the England job. Now being guided by Ruud Gullit, Dennis is still producing the goods on a regular basis, with his forward runs enabling Mark Hughes and Gianluca Vialli to have more freedom of movement. Gullit must be grateful that he inherited a midfielder who can guarantee 15 goals per season.

Chelsea
STATS AND FACTS

Manager: **Ruud Gullit**
Captain: **Dennis Wise**
Colours: **Home -**
Royal Blue and White
Away -
Yellow and Sky Blue
Ground: **Stamford Bridge**

CLUB HONOURS

LEAGUE
Champions: 1954-55

FA CUP
Winners: 1970

LEAGUE CUP
Winners: 1965

EUROPEAN CUP WINNERS' CUP
Winners: 1971

INS AND OUTS

INS	OUTS
Gianluca Vialli **Juventus**	Nigel Spackman **Sheffield Utd**
Roberto Di Matteo **Lazio**	Paul Furlong **Birmingham**
Frank Leboeuf **Strasbourg**	Mustafa Izzet **Leicester**
	Zeke Rowe **Peterborough**
	Anthony Barness **Charlton**

TITLE ODDS
20/1
ON AUGUST 17th, START OF SEASON

What are their chances?

With changes galore over the summer, Chelsea are on course for a very interesting and exciting season. Glenn Hoddle's departure has let in Ruud Gullit, who will bring a whole new era to Chelsea – their style of play will become more continental and, with quality players such as Roberto di Matteo and Gianluca Vialli, they will score goals. This season is the start of a revival at Stamford Bridge and even if the trophies do not come this year, the Chelsea fans can be promised some fantastic football.

INTERNATIONAL PLAYERS

(above)
Dmitri Kharine
Russia

■

Dan Petrescu
Romania

■

Frank Leboeuf
France

■

John Spencer
Scotland

■

Mark Hughes
Wales

■

Roberto Di Matteo
Italy

■

Erland Johnson
Norway

■

Terry Phelan
Eire

1 KHARINE

6 CLARKE **5** LEBOEUF **18** JOHNSON

2 PETRESCU **3** PHELAN

11 WISE **16** DI MATTEO **4** GULLIT

9 VIALLI **10** HUGHES

TEAM POSITIONS AND LINE–UP

1	Dmitri Kharine (GK)	14 Craig Burley
2	Dan Petrescu	15 David Lee
3	Terry Phelan	16 Roberto Di Matteo
4	Ruud Gullit	17 Scott Minto
5	Frank Leboeuf	18 Erland Johnson
6	Steve Clarke	19 Gavin Peacock
7	John Spencer	20 Frank Sinclair
8	Andy Myers	21 Jody Morris
9	Gianluca Vialli	22 Mark Nicholls
10	Mark Hughes	
11	Dennis Wise	
12	Michael Duberry	
13	Kevin Hitchcock (GK)	

Gavin Peacock

Frank Sinclair

David Burrows
Defender

Place of Birth   **Dudley, England**
Height   1.78m
Date of Birth   25-10-68
Weight   73kg

Tough tackling David is now playing under Ron Atkinson after two seasons of moving around England! David made 150 appearances for Liverpoool, gaining an England 'B' cap. But, after not fitting into Graeme Souness' plans he moved south to join West Ham where he was successful but unsettled. A year later he moved to Everton, but after only 20 games 'Bugsy' was on the move again.

Big Ron splashed out £1.5m on David; he seems to have settled and the tough defender plays a big part in Coventry's Premiership survival.

Gordon Strachan
Midfielder

Place of Birth   **Edinburgh, Scotland**
Height   1.68m
Date of Birth   09-02-57
Weight   66kg

The silky Scot has at last begun to wind down his career and has been lined up to try his luck at management at Coventry City, and he could not have learned under a better manager than Big Ron Atkinson.

Gordon first came into the limelight under the same man, during Manchester United's 1985 FA Cup, when they beat Everton in the final. He was rewarded by being selected for Scotland in two World Cups, where he shone because of his small frame but big heart.

Paul Telfer
Midfielder

Place of Birth   Edinburgh, Scotland
Height   1.75m
Date of Birth   21-10-71
Weight   72kg

The highlight of Paul's career must have been his Wembley appearance for Luton against Chelsea in the 1994 FA Cup semi-final. Luton may have lost the match, but Paul certainly attracted attention. Many clubs were chasing his signature, but wisely he chose to join Ron Atkinson's Coventry revolution. Alongside Gary MacAllister and Liam Daish, Paul will be hoping his midfield performances will at least be rewarded with a place in Europe.

In addition, Paul is still young and it can only be a matter of time until he is presented with an international call-up.

John Salako
Striker

Place of Birth	Nigeria
Height	1.75m
Date of Birth	11-02-69
Weight	78kg

Born in Nigeria, John was an apprentice at Crystal Palace where he made over 200 appearances. After making a real impact and pushing himself into the England squad five years ago, an injury then threatened his career.

John bounced right back, regaining his form straight away, but was then lured to Highfield Road where his form has been somewhat indifferent.

Now John hopes to become part of Glenn Hoddle's plans and take a place in the squad for World Cup 98.

Dion Dublin
Striker

Place of Birth	Leicester, England
Height	1.88m
Date of Birth	22-04-69
Weight	78kg

Having established himself as one of the top strikers in the Premiership, he richly deserves credit from his club.

He would never have dreamt three years ago, as he sat in the Manchester United reserves, that he would now be captain of Coventry.

His goalscoring record speaks for itself – 27 goals in 65 appearances make him Coventry's top scorer since he joined.

Peter Ndlovu
Striker

Place of Birth	Bulawayo, Zimbabwe
Height	1.73m
Date of Birth	25-02-73
Weight	64kg

While last season was one of mixed endeavours and mixed performances, Peter is still one of the most skilled players with some of the best skill in the Premiership and has much to offer Coventry City.

With new arrivals last season along with Ron Atkinson's chopping and changing, Peter found it hard to get a settled place and position in the team.

The Zimbabwian international has a tremendous attitude towards the game and with his mixture of strength and ability, he can prove a real handful for defenders.

Coventry City

STATS AND FACTS

Manager: Ron Atkinson

Captain: Dion Dublin

Colours: Home - Sky Blue and Navy
Away - Red and Navy

Ground: Highfield Road

TITLE ODDS
150/1
ON AUGUST 17th,
START OF SEASON

CLUB HONOURS

FA CUP
Winners: 1987

What are their chances?

The £3 million arrival of Gary McAllister is the most significant step in Coventry's progress and ambition to become one of the big boys in Premiership football.
Their team has a good blend of youth and experience, yet the players' talents are of such varied ability that they may find it difficult to stay on the same wavelength.
Coventry will avoid a relegation battle this year, but a mid-table position is all that can be hoped for.

INS AND OUTS

INS	OUTS
Gary McAllister *Leeds*	David Rennie *Northampton*
Michael O'Neill *Hibs*	Lee Hirst *unsigned*
Regis Genaux *Std. Liege*	Ally Pickering *Stoke*
	Jonathan Gould *Bradford*

Dion Dublin

24

INTERNATIONAL PLAYERS

Eoin Jess
Scotland

■

Gary McAllister
Scotland

■

Peter Ndlovu
Zimbabwe

■

Regis Genaux
Belgium

TEAM POSITIONS AND LINE-UP

1	Steve Ogrizovic (GK)	**14**	Peter Ndlovu
2	Richard Shaw	**15**	Marques Isaias
3	David Burrows	**16**	Brian Borrows
4	Paul Williams	**17**	Willie Boland
5	Liam Daish	**18**	Marcus Hall
6	Kevin Richardson	**19**	Iyseden Christie
7	Eoin Jess	**20**	Michael O'Neill
8	Noel Whelan	**21**	Andrew Ducros
9	Dion Dublin	**22**	Gavin O'Toole
10	Gary McAllister	**24**	Regis Genaux
11	John Salako	**26**	Gordon Strachan
12	Paul Telfer	**30**	Lorcan Costello
13	John Filan (GK)		

Chris Powell
Defender

Place of Birth	London, England
Height	1.78m
Date of Birth	08-09-69
Weight	73kg

After being transferred from Southend United last season, it took time for Chris to settle in and justify the £800,000 Jim Smith paid for him. Having familiarised himself with the Derby style, he won the fans over with his pacey runs down the wing and dangerous crosses.

Chris was a player who attracted a lot of attraction from Premiership sides, including Tottenham and West Ham, but it seemed Derby were there first and what a find he has been.

Igor Stimac
Defender

Place of Birth	Croatia
Height	1.88m
Date of Birth	06-09-67
Weight	83kg

The sturdy centre back made a great impact at the Baseball Ground last season.

The Croatian international not only played a major part in helping Derby gain promotion, but he was also influential in helping Croatia reach the quarter final of the European Championships. A solid defender who likes to come forward and score goals, Igor is a player who is sure to adapt from playing nationwide league football to playing in the Premiership.

Darryl Powell
Defender

Place of Birth	London, England
Height	1.85m
Date of Birth	15-01-71
Weight	71kg

Jim Smith obviously realised that a strong midfield is required to compete in the Premiership. Due to several new additions to the squad, he can now choose from players like Asanovic, Simpson, Flynn, Dailly and Powell.

Darryl was signed from Portsmouth and is extremely useful breaking through from midfield into the attacking third.

The Premiership defenders are likely to be much tougher than the Derby strikers are used to, and Jim will therefore be relying on players like Powell to ensure Premiership survival.

Robin Van der Laan
Midfielder

Place of Birth	Schiedam, The Netherlands
Height	1.80m
Date of Birth	05-09-68
Weight	86kg

Before each game, Robin hears all the jokes from the opposition fans about his unusual hair style. However, he answers back in the best possible way, as he thrives on his attacking midfield role and scores many more goals than people expect.

Robin has been at Derby all of his English career, and he is a vital cog in the wheel that attempts to turn defence into attack. His speed off the mark is essential as the Baseball Ground side look to counter-attack when the opposition are not ready. Premiership defences are warned to ignore Robin at their peril!

Aljosa Asanovic
Midfielder

Place of Birth	Split, Croatia
Height	1.83m
Date of Birth	14-12-65
Weight	78kg

As one of the bargains of the close season, Jim Smith was obviously aware of the ability that Asanovic possessed long before the European Championships.

His performance in the Championships was quite astounding, his passing being second to none. He played a major part in helping Croatia to the quarter finals.

This attacking midfielder is sure to be a great success and join fellow countrymen, Stimac and Bilic, in flying the flag for Croatia.

Paul Simpson
Striker

Place of Birth	Carlisle, England
Height	1.68m
Date of Birth	26-06-66
Weight	74kg

The winger with the magical left foot has at long last been rewarded with the chance to show exactly what he can do in the top flight. He was signed by Derby in the early 1990s from Manchester City, where the fans were outraged to see their favourite allowed to leave for such a small fee.

He was part of Derby's relegation side the following season, but throughput the last five seasons he has been the side's spot-kick specialist. His free-kicks and breaks down the left flank mean that he is a regular supplier of 15 goals a year.

There is little doubt that Derby will need this supply of goals if they are to stay in the top division and avoid an early return to the Nationwide League.

Derby County

STATS AND FACTS

Manager: Jim Smith
Captain: Igor Stimac
Colours: Home - White and Black
Away - Maroon and White
Ground: Baseball Ground

INS AND OUTS

INS	OUTS
Aljosa Asanovic Hajduk Split	**Darren Wrack** Grimsby
Jakob Laursen Silkeborg	
Christian Dailly Dundee United	
Paul Parker Manchester Utd	

TITLE ODDS

250/1

ON AUGUST 17th,
START OF SEASON

CLUB HONOURS

LEAGUE CHAMPIONS
1971-72, 1974-75

FA CUP
Winners: 1946

What are their chances?

Newly-promoted Derby had been tipped for a speedy return to the 1st Division, but boss Jim Smith has brought in many fresh and talented faces.
The skill of Asanovic and strength of Stimac give Derby solid foundations, with the two Croatians playing a major role in both defending and attacking options.
Survival is the main ambition for Jim Smith and his side, and they have enough quality players to stay in the Premiership.

TEAM POSITIONS AND LINE-UP

1	Russell Hoult (GK)	14	Paul Simpson
2	Gary Rowett	15	Paul Trollope
3	Chris Powell	16	Jakob Laursen
4	Darryl Powell	17	Matthew Carbon
5	Dean Yates	18	Lee Carsley
6	Igor Stimac	19	Sean Flynn
7	Robin Van der Laan	20	Darren Wassall
8	Dean Sturridge	21	Jason Kavanagh
9	Ashley Ward	22	Christian Dailly
10	Aljosa Asanovic	23	Paul Parker
11	Ron Willems		
12	Marco Gabbiadini		
13	Steve Sutton (GK)		

INTERNATIONAL PLAYERS

Igor Stimac
Croatia

•

Jakob Laursen
Denmark

•

Aljosa Asanovic
Croatia
(below)

Dave Watson
Defender

Place of Birth	Liverpool, England
Height	1.83m
Date of Birth	20–11–61
Weight	86kg

Dave is to Everton what Tony Adams is to Arsenal or what Stuart Pearce is to Nottingham Forest – an experienced and inspirational leader who gives 100% commitment every time he steps onto the pitch.

Joe Royle is fortunate enough to have many talented defenders at his disposal, players such as Unsworth, Short and Barrett. However, it is a credit to Dave that, at his age, he is still one of the first names on his manager's team sheet every week.

Dave realises he is coming to the end of his career and this has fired his determination to collect more silverware in Everton's colours. Dave's qualities as a defender ensure that Everton are a hard team to score against and with players such as Kanchelskis and Ferguson on the attacking front, Dave's dream may well come true.

Neville Southall
Goalkeeper

Place of Birth	Llandudno, Wales
Height	1.83m
Date of Birth	16–09–58
Weight	89kg

Having just made his 700th appearance for the club, many Evertonians thought that this season would be his last at Goodison Park. New signing, Paul Gerrard has come in and is putting pressure on the big shot-stopper, but Neville is standing firm.

Neville is still instrumental in the success of the Welsh national side, and is intending to guide them to the World Cup in France in 1998, which will probably signal a fitting end of his playing career. There will, no doubt, be a number of managerial jobs awaiting him, and he will be in the enviable position of being able to pick and choose where he goes.

David Unsworth
Defender

Place of Birth	Preston, England
Height	1.83m
Date of Birth	16–10–73
Weight	89kg

Although Joe Royle splashed out over £2 million to Derby for Craig Short, and has Dave Watson as a reliable and experienced veteran, it is a member of the Goodison Park youth scheme who is the rock around which Joe's defence is built. It must come as a bonus that David also feels comfortable taking penalties for the Everton team.

David earned his first cap for England in the 1995 Umbro Cup and, with Tony Adams and Gary Pallister showing their age, David is clearly the future of the England set-up.

Gary Speed
Midfielder

Place of Birth   Hawarden, England
Height   1.75m
Date of Birth   08-09-69
Weight   81kg

After a disappointing season for Leeds, through injury and lack of form, Gary is looking forward to his new challenge at Everton. Both Howard Wilkinson and Joe Royle are in the process of rebuilding their sides, and what was no longer required at Leeds was certainly welcomed at Everton.

Gary is an energetic player who is not frightened to put his foot in and, like David Platt, he is a midfielder with the knack of being in the right place at the right time, enabling him to keep adding to his goal tally. Gary is a recognised Welsh international and, with prices inflating in the present-day market, Joe Royle seems to have made a bargain buy, paying around £3.5 million for Gary.

Duncan Ferguson
Striker

Place of Birth   Stirling, Scotland
Height   1.90m
Date of Birth   27-12-71
Weight   86kg

After his brief spell in jail, Duncan is now the perfect role model to anyone who is fighting personal anguish. He has put his 'Duncan Disorderly' days firmly behind him, and is finally recognised as one of the Premiership's most exciting and prolific strikers.

Duncan has always praised his manager, Joe Royle, who took a huge risk when he decided to bring him down to England from Glasgow Rangers in a £4 million-plus deal. After a troublesome first year, his faith has been firmly rewarded as Everton begin to build on their 95/96 sixth place to secure a place in Europe.

Andrei Kanchelskis
Striker

Place of Birth   Kirovograd, Ukraine
Height   1.78m
Date of Birth   23-01-69
Weight   82kg

The Flying Russian's move to Goodison Park nearly collapsed a year ago, but it looks as though the struggle to sign him has paid off for Everton. He has settled in fine at Everton and his unsettled times are over – especially since he managed to become top scorer in the 95/96 campaign. Hopefully, Andrei will not start the season the way he finished Euro 96, where he was on disappointing form.

Everton
STATS AND FACTS

Manager: Joe Royle
Captain: Dave Watson
Colours: Home - Royal Blue and White
Away - Amber and Black
Ground: Goodison Park

CLUB HONOURS

LEAGUE
Champions:
1890–91, 1914–15,
1927–28, 1931–32,
1938–39, 1962–63,
1969–70, 1984–85,
1986–87

FA CUP
Winners: 1906, 1933, 1966,
1984, 1995

EUROPEAN CUP WINNERS' CUP
Winners: 1985

What are their chances?

Joe Royle has built a team that is strong, big and resilient, yet it lacks flair. Could this prove to be the reason if they fail to challenge at the end of the season?
Gary Speed will add pace and determination to Andrei Kanchelskis' play, and much is expected of Duncan Ferguson in his first full season in the Premiership.
A good cup team, Everton will be hard to beat; yet they will find it difficult to score goals, unless they find a quality striker to partner Ferguson.

INS AND OUTS

INS	OUTS
Gary Speed **Leeds Utd**	Gary Ablett **Birmingham**
Paul Gerrard **Oldham**	Barry Horne **Birmingham**
	Daniel Amokachi **Besiktas**

32

INTERNATIONAL PLAYERS

Neville Southall
Wales

▪

Andy Hinchcliffe
England

▪

Duncan Ferguson
Scotland

▪

Gary Speed
Wales

▪

Andrei Kanchelskis
Russia

▪

Marc Hottiger
Switzerland

▪

Anders Limpar
Sweden

(below)

TEAM POSITIONS AND LINE–UP

1	Neville Southall (GK)	20	Tony Grant
2	Earl Barrett	21	Craig Short
3	Andy Hinchcliffe	22	Peter Holcroft
4	David Unsworth	23	Michael Branch
5	Dave Watson	24	Jonathan O'Connor
7	Graham Stuart	25	Neil Moore
8	Paul Rideout	26	Graham Allen
9	Duncan Ferguson	27	Mark Grugel
10	Gary Speed	28	Chris Price
11	Anders Limpar	29	Gavin McCann
13	Jason Kearton (GK)	30	Richard Townsend
14	John Ebbrell	31	Paul Gerrard (GK)
15	Matthew Jackson	32	Robert Tynan
16	Vinny Samways	33	James Speare (GK)
17	Andrei Kanchelskis	34	Edward Hussin
18	Joe Parkinson	35	John Hills
19	Marc Hottiger		

Carlton Palmer
Defender

Place of Birth	Oldbun, England
Height	1.90m
Date of Birth	05-12-65
Weight	82kg

Often the brunt of opposition supporters' jokes after a couple of disappointing performances for England under Graham Taylor, Carlton has matured significantly and is now one of the country's most improved central midfielders. He has also adapted more easily than other players to the new role of 'sweeper', which many club managers are now deploying.

Glenn Hoddle will be noting his performances and, if Paul Ince is injured or suspended, then England could do a lot worse than give Carlton a chance to resurrect his international career.

Lee Bowyer
Midfielder

Place of Birth	London, England
Height	1.75m
Date of Birth	03-01-77
Weight	61kg

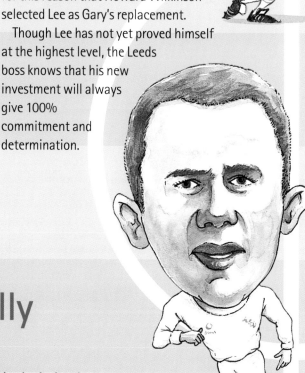

After returning to the game from his FA ban, Lee managed to become the 'shining star' among the group of youngsters guided by Alan Curbishley at Charlton Athletic.

Like Gary Speed on form, he is full of energy and has a vicious shot – and it was for this reason that Howard Wilkinson selected Lee as Gary's replacement.

Though Lee has not yet proved himself at the highest level, the Leeds boss knows that his new investment will always give 100% commitment and determination.

Gary Kelly
Defender

Place of Birth	Drogheda, Ireland
Height	1.75m
Date of Birth	09-07-74
Weight	70kg

He was always full of promise and has performed well. Unfortunately Leeds failed to attain the same level of play as Gary.

He has clocked up over 120 appearances for Leeds and is also becoming a regular in the Republic of Ireland side; so at only 22, he seems to have his career sewn up already.

Gary is part of the very successful youth policy that is providing Leeds with many talented and strong individuals, and if future players can match Gary's standards they are in for good times at Elland Road.

Rod Wallace
Midfielder

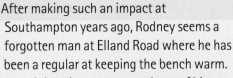

Place of Birth	Lewisham, England
Height	1.70m
Date of Birth	02-10-69
Weight	73kg

After making such an impact at Southampton years ago, Rodney seems a forgotten man at Elland Road where he has been a regular at keeping the bench warm.

It is a shame to see a player of his ability and ambition failing to play a major part in the Premiership.

With a new season and new manager ahead of him, Rodney may make a fresh start at Elland Road. Perhaps he can recapture his Southampton glory days with some dazzling performances?

Tony Yeboah
Striker

Place of Birth	Kumasi, Ghana
Height	1.80m
Date of Birth	06-06-66
Weight	93kg

On form, Tony is as good as any striker in the world. His entrance into English football was nothing less than remarkable. However, 1996 was not a good year for Tony or Leeds; commitments to his national side, Ghana, meant he was immediately ruled out for a month of Premiership football even before he picked up a long-term injury.

It is no surprise that Leeds' massive dip in performance coincided with Tony's absence from the team.

Leeds are currently in a transitional period, looking for some sort of consistency, so both the Elland Road faithful and new boss, George Graham, will be looking to Tony to provide some answers.

There is certainly a great deal of pressure on Tony's shoulders, but that is just part of being a great player and if anyone is capable of responding in dramatic fashion, it is him.

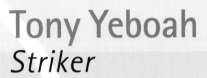

Ian Rush
Striker

Place of Birth	St Asaph, Wales
Height	1.83m
Date of Birth	20-10-61
Weight	79kg

Even though he has lost some pace and does not have the stamina he used to, Ian Rush is still feared by many Premiership defenders because of his deadly goal scoring ability.

After spending a total of 10 years at Liverpool, he broke many goal scoring records, yet his place seemed threatened by Robbie Fowler and Stan Collymore, and he felt that he was too good for a place on the bench.

Now at Leeds, he has a fresh challenge in partnering Tony Yeboah, and helping Leeds find some league consistency.

Leeds United

STATS AND FACTS

What are their chances?

Leeds have taken a massive gamble replacing stalwarts Speed and McAllister with fresh faces, such as Bowyer and Sharpe, yet they are looking to the future in a big way.
Their squad is full of promising youngsters – Gray, Couzens, Harte and Tinkler to name but a few, and there is also experience with Ian Rush and Carlton Palmer in the squad.
The Leeds' fans expect trophies and demand success; this season will possibly lay the foundation for future triumphs.

CLUB HONOURS

LEAGUE
Champions: 1968–69, 1973–74, 1991–92

FA CUP
Winners: 1972

LEAGUE CUP
Winners: 1968

INS AND OUTS

INS	OUTS
Ian Rush **Liverpool**	Gary McAllister **Coventry**
Lee Bowyer **Charlton**	Gary Speed **Everton**
Lee Sharpe **Manchester Utd**	Phil Masinga **St Gallen**
Nigel Martyn **Crystal Palace**	Nigel Worthington **Stoke**
	John Lukic **Arsenal**

Manager: George Graham
Captain: Carlton Palmer
Colours:
Home - White, Blue and Yellow
Away - Yellow, White and Blue
Ground: Elland Road

TITLE ODDS
66/1
ON AUGUST 17th, START OF SEASON

INTERNATIONAL PLAYERS

Gary Kelly
Eire

•

Lucas Radebe
S. Africa

•

Ian Rush
Wales

•

Tony Yeboah
Ghana

1 MARTYN

6 WETHERALL   **16** JOBSON

2 KELLY   **4** PALMER   **3** DORIGO

7 SHARPE   **11** BOWYER   **14** GRAY

9 RUSH   **21** YEBOAH

TEAM POSITIONS AND LINE-UP

1	Nigel Martyn (GK)	19	Harry Kewell
2	Gary Kelly	20	Ian Harte
3	Tony Dorigo	21	Tony Yeboah
4	Carlton Palmer	22	Mark Ford
5	Lucas Radebe	23	Andrew Couzens
6	David Wetherall	24	Jason Blunt
7	Lee Sharpe	25	Robert Bowman
8	Rod Wallace	26	Paul Beesley
9	Ian Rush	27	Alan Maybury
10	Brian Deane	28	Paul Shepherd
11	Lee Bowyer	29	Mark Jackson
12	John Pemberton	31	Martin Foster
14	Andrew Gray	32	Andrew Wright
15	Mark Beeney (GK)	34	Paul Evans
16	Richard Jobson	35	Lawrence Davies
17	Mark Tinkler	36	Tomas Brolin

Steve Walsh
Defender

Place of Birth	Fulwood, England
Height	1.90m
Date of Birth	03-11-64
Weight	92kg

When one thinks of Leicester City, Steve Walsh immediately comes to mind.

He is a typical 'hard' English centre half, but his dependability and influence are second to none. He was a key reason for Leicester's promotion, and now that they are back in the Premiership, strikers must beware. Likewise, Steve is also known for his usefulness in the opposition's penalty box; he is a man to be feared all over the pitch.

Julian Watts
Defender

Place of Birth	Sheffield, England
Height	1.90m
Date of Birth	17-03-71
Weight	86kg

Julian was unable to command a place in the Sheffield Wednesday defence, and was available for Martin O'Neill to snap up in their bid to regain Premiership status.

He never seemed an accomplished defender in the Premiership, yet the nine games he played for Leicester proved he was a success in the First Division during Leicester's push for the play-offs.

He will find it hard in the Premiership; we will just have to wait and see whether he will be able to cope as well as he did in the First Division.

Simon Grayson
Defender

Place of Birth	Ripon, England
Height	1.83m
Date of Birth	16-12-69
Weight	79kg

Typical of Leicester's promotion winning team, Simon is a solid defender who can either effectively mark another player man-to-man, or can simply be left to play like a natural defender.

Since Martin O'Neill took over at Filbert Street, he has brought in many new faces, but Simon's consistency has ensured that he maintained his position.

However, like so many others, Simon realises that the Premiership is an entirely new challenge, which he will have to rise to if he wants to be involved on a weekly basis.

Neil Lennon
Midfielder

Place of Birth	Lurgan, Ireland
Height	1.78m
Date of Birth	25–06–71
Weight	82kg

Neil made a name for himself in the lower divisions with Crewe Alexandra where he consistently put in good performances. He caught the eye of many top clubs including Coventry, but opted for a move to Leicester. He made an immediate impact, bringing strength to an already impressive midfield.

He now has the chance to prove himself at the highest level – a task he should not find too daunting, having already established himself on the international scene with Northern Ireland. Neil has often been compared to David Batty, but his goal-scoring record is much better.

Garry Parker
Midfielder

Place of Birth	Oxford, England
Height	1.83m
Date of Birth	07–09–65
Weight	83kg

Garry's great skills and passing ability have made him an important part of the former Nottingham Forest and Aston Villa teams.

There was some surprise when Garry decided to join Leicester for the 1994/95 campaign. However, he clearly recognised the team's potential, and contributed to their promotion in 1996 with a decisive penalty kick in the play-off final against Crystal Palace. Garry, like Steve Bruce, is a quality player who has never been capped by his country.

Steve Claridge
Striker

Place of Birth	Portsmouth, England
Height	1.83m
Date of Birth	10–04–66
Weight	81kg

Steve is not the most naturally-gifted footballer in the world, but is still every manager's dream. He works tirelessly in each game he plays, and strives for team success ahead of individual success.

Martin O'Neill bought Steve late on in the 95/96 campaign to provide greater fire-power in his team's search for promotion. Steve pitched in with some vital goals, none more so than the dramatic last-minute winner in the play-off final, which sent Leicester into the top flight.

Leicester City

STATS AND FACTS

Manager: Martin O'Neill
Captain: Steve Walsh
Colours: Home - Royal Blue and White
Away - Jade and Navy
Ground: Filbert Street

CLUB HONOURS

LEAGUE CUP
Winners: 1964

Martin O'Neill

What are their chances?

Rank outsiders Leicester seem to be destined for the drop. Their yo-yo status between the 1st Division and the Premiership may keep fans excited, yet there has not been stability at the club for years.

With very little money available, Martin O'Neill must rely heavily on the team that brought Leicester up. Players that will make their name in the Premiership are the exciting Emile Heskey and the tenacious Neil Lennon; even though they won't prevent the inevitable relegation.

INS AND OUTS

INS	OUTS
Mustafa Izzet Chelsea	Brian Carey Wrexham
	Iwan Roberts Wolves

40

INTERNATIONAL PLAYERS

Neil Lennon
N. Ireland

TEAM POSITIONS AND LINE-UP

1	Kasey Keller (GK)	14	Colin Hill
2	Simon Grayson	15	Pontus Kamark
3	Mike Whitlow	16	Frank Rolling
4	Julian Watts	21	Jamie Lawrence
5	Steve Walsh	22	Neil Lewis
6	Mustafa Izzet	23	Sam McMahon
7	Neil Lennon	24	Jimmy Willis
8	Scott Taylor		
9	Steve Claridge		
10	Garry Parker		
11	Emile Heskey		
12	Mark Robins		

David James
Goalkeeper

Place of Birth	Welwyn, Wales
Height	1.95m
Date of Birth	01-08-70
Weight	90kg

When David was bought from Watford in a multi-million pound deal, he was considered inexperienced and unable to fill the gloves of Bruce Grobbelaar.

After two seasons, David is recognised as one of the top goalkeepers in the country; his handling is quite superb and he is probably the best keeper in the country for saving crosses. He has earned himself a place in the England team, having been picked for the first World Cup qualifying squad; it looks as though it will be a battle between David and Ian Walker to take Seaman's shirt.

Jamie Redknapp
Midfielder

Place of Birth	Barton-on-Sea, England
Height	1.83m
Date of Birth	25-06-73
Weight	81kg

Since the closing months of the 95/96 campaign, Jamie's continual injury problems have been frustrating both for himself, his team and his country. Though still young, he has enormous potential and is a player who can only add to a team's performance.

When Terry Venables introduced Jamie into the European Championship game against Scotland there was an immediate improvement in the team's style and attitude. Unfortunately, in the very same game, Jamie picked up the knock which halted his comeback. Liverpool manager, Roy Evans, knows that if he is to bring the title back to Anfield this season, he will need Jamie Redknapp in the heart of midfield – dominating the game as he so often does.

Jason McAteer
Midfielder

Place of Birth	Birkenhead, England
Height	1.80m
Date of Birth	18-06-71
Weight	74kg

Roy Evans made Jason wait for his debut in Liverpool's colours, but since then the Republic of Ireland international has never looked back, and has established himself as possibly the best attacking wing back in the British Isles.

People often find it hard to decide whether he is a defender or a midfielder, but he is equally comfortable tackling back in his own box or whipping in a cross to the opponent's area.

Along with his best friend, Alan Stubbs, he was the basis of Bolton's 1995 promotion side, but it was always expected that he would eventually move to a bigger club.

Stan Collymore
Striker

Place of Birth	Stone, England
Height	1.88m
Date of Birth	22-01-71
Weight	89kg

Although 'Stan the Man' is still finding it hard to settle on Merseyside, the Kop have established him as a firm favourite of theirs, and the number of quality goals he scores is beginning to pay back the huge £8.5 million paid to Nottingham Forest. Roy Evans will be more impressed by Stan's tremendous work-rate, and he is often seen out on the wings, supplying ammunition for Robbie Fowler to steal the headlines. He may be an unsung hero, but he is without doubt a striker that every manager would love to have in their team.

Robbie Fowler
Striker

Place of Birth	Liverpool, England
Height	1.80m
Date of Birth	09-04-75
Weight	74kg

Liverpool have the knack of finding great strikers – Keegan, Dalglish and Rush all come to mind – and once again they have not disappointed with their new find, Robbie Fowler.

At present, there are many top strikers in English football, but Robbie has been singled out as something special. Not only did Robbie net 28 goals in the 95/96 campaign, but he repeatedly showed flashes of brilliance. As a result, he was rewarded with an international call-up.

Some worry that the apparent problems between Robbie's striking partner, Collymore, and the club might unsettle Robbie and the other younger players. It is therefore ironic that on many occasions it is Robbie's goals and performance that stabilise the team.

Steve McManaman
Striker

Place of Birth	Liverpool, England
Height	1.83m
Date of Birth	11-02-72
Weight	66kg

At only 24 years old, it seems as if Steve has been in the game for decades. His experience of top-level football is now unrivalled and, mixed with his passion and skill, what a player this makes him!

Last season proved one of the most successful for Steve, and he is now regarded as one of the top ten players in the world. After very impressive Euro 96 performances, Steve goes into this season with much expected of him. His confidence is as good as his ability; he could play a major part in Liverpool's success this season.

Liverpool

STATS AND FACTS

CLUB HONOURS

LEAGUE
Champions: 1900–01,
1905–06, 1921–22,
1922–23, 1946–47,
1963–64, 1965–66,
1972–73, 1975–76,
1976–77, 1978–79,
1979–80, 1981–82,
1982–83, 1983–84,
1985–86, 1987–88,
1989–90

FA CUP
Winners: 1965, 1974, 1986,
1989, 1992

LEAGUE CUP
Winners: 1981, 1982,
1983, 1984, 1995

EUROPEAN CUP
Winners: 1977,
1978, 1981, 1984

EUROPEAN SUPER CUP
Winners: 1977

Manager: Roy Evans
Captain: John Barnes
Colours: Home - Red
Away - Ecru and Black
Ground: Anfield

INS AND OUTS

INS	OUTS
Patrik Berger Borussia Dortmund	Ian Rush Leeds

What are their chances?

Roy Evans and his side mount a major challenge to the title this year, with a side which has now matured in strength and vision, and is capable of winning trophies.
The partnership of Collymore and Fowler is possibly the most balanced in the Premiership and with such talent as Redknapp, McManaman and the impressive Berger, they look formidable. They are good enough to win the Cup Winners' Cup, but should not let this distract them from their Championship challenge.

TEAM POSITIONS AND LINE-UP

1	David James (GK)	13	Anthony Warner (GK)
2	Rob Jones	14	Neil Ruddock
3	John Scales	15	Patrik Berger
4	Jason McAteer	16	Michael Thomas
5	Mark Wright	18	Phil Charnock
6	Phil Babb	19	Mark Kennedy
7	Steve McManaman	20	Stig Inge Bjornebye
8	Stan Collymore	21	Dominic Matteo
9	Robbie Fowler	23	James Carragher
10	John Barnes	24	Lee Jones
11	Jamie Redknapp	25	David Thompson
12	Steve Harkness		

Peter Schmeichel
Goalkeeper

Place of Birth	Gladsaxe, Denmark
Height	1.93m
Date of Birth	18-11-63
Weight	101kg

Gary Pallister
Defender

Place of Birth	Ramsgate, England
Height	1.93m
Date of Birth	30-06-65
Weight	95kg

The England centre back is gradually recovering from the persistent back problems that plagued him throughout Manchester United's double success of 95/96. Alongside David May, Alex Ferguson will be desperate for Gary to continue his high-level of play as the Old Trafford team intend to add even more silverware to their trophy cabinet.

Signed from Middlesbrough in 1989, Gary took time to show his value, but once he was given a full run in the team it was obvious that he was set to be a star for the future.

The 'Great Dane' was one of the most outstanding players of the 95/96 campaign. His heroics inspired confidence throughout the Manchester United team and helped win them the title.

Peter is hailed as one of the greatest goalkeepers in the world, with his strength and presence behind any defence giving reassurance to the rest of the team.

Having been disappointed with his performance in Euro 96, Peter's enthusiasm for the game is back on course as the new season dawns.

Roy Keane
Midfielder

Place of Birth	Cork, Ireland
Height	1.78m
Date of Birth	10-08-71
Weight	81kg

Bryan Robson once described Roy as the most complete midfielder in British football. Therefore, it is not surprising that Bryan's namesake, Bobby, made an audacious bid for the Republic of Ireland star in the summer of 1996, in an attempt to lure the player away to the bright lights of Barcelona. It is also not surprising that Alex Ferguson offered Roy an improved contract in order to keep him, putting him on a par with the other top players in the English game.

Roy's drive and determination from the heart of the midfield are reminiscent of Paul Ince, and Alex Ferguson knows that in order to bring the European Cup back to Old Trafford, Roy will need to be on top form. His start to the 96/97 campaign – for instance his performance in the Charity Shield – can only be looked on in a positive light.

Ryan Giggs
Striker

Place of Birth	Cardiff, Wales
Height	1.80m
Date of Birth	29-11-73
Weight	67kg

Wonderkid Ryan has been *the* boyhood sensation; now, with new up-and-coming players arriving on the scene Ryan is regarded as an experienced player!

Giggsy's flashes of skill and amazing ability were recaptured last season after it seemed as though his best form was gone.

The 'Boy Wonder' is now always assured of his first team place, and his talent will be something to contend with – especially with the support of new players around him.

Eric Cantona
Striker

Place of Birth	Paris, France
Height	1.88m
Date of Birth	24-05-66
Weight	90kg

Many critics believed that Eric did not have the right temperament to cope with his year-long ban. When he returned in October 1996, not only did he prove those people wrong, but he did so in sensational fashion.

Eric's 95/96 campaign was undoubtedly his most successful since making his debut in English football. He spearheaded Manchester United's attack, to the famous 'double double', and he collected the 'Player of the Year' award. His magic was as inspirational as ever, his goals were even more consistent, and his vast improvement in attitude was rewarded by Alex Ferguson when he made Eric captain towards the latter stages of the season.

Eric Cantona has now established himself as one of the great players in the world, and it seems absurd that he was not picked for France's squad for the European Championships – even if it meant disrupting the French system.

David Beckham
Midfielder

Place of Birth	Leytonstone, England
Height	1.83m
Date of Birth	02-05-75
Weight	71kg

Leytonstone born, and without a doubt the real star of the early part of the 95/96 season, David has got a tremendous career ahead of him. The game against Moldova – England's first World Cup qualifier – saw David's early-season form rewarded with an international call-up. In 1995, he was noticed for his tireless performances in the Old Trafford midfield, but more recently his all-round skills have developed. His individual display in the Charity Shield against Newcastle was the best to grace Wembley for a long time, and both Alex Ferguson and Glenn Hoddle agree that they have a real gem on their hands.

STATS AND FACTS

Manager: Alex Ferguson
Captain: Eric Cantona
Colours: Home - Red and White
Away - White
Ground: Old Trafford

CLUB HONOURS

LEAGUE
Champions: 1907–08, 1910–11, 1951–52, 1955–56, 1956–57, 1964–65, 1966–67, 1992–1993, 1993–94, 1995–96

FA CUP
Winners: 1909, 1948, 1963, 1977, 1983, 1985, 1990, 1994, 1996

LEAGUE CUP
Winners: 1992

EUROPEAN CUP WINNERS' CUP
Winners: 1991

EUROPEAN SUPER CUP
Winners: 1991

INS AND OUTS

INS	OUTS
Ronny Johnsen **Besiktas**	Steve Bruce **Birmingham**
Ole Gunnar Solskjaer **Moide**	Paul Parker **Derby**
Raimond vaan der Gouw **Vitesse Arnhem**	Tony Coton **Sunderland**
Karel Poborsky **Slavia Prague**	Lee Sharpe **Leeds**
Jordi Cruyff **Barcelona**	

TITLE ODDS

6/4

ON AUGUST 17th, START OF SEASON

What are their chances?

After such a fantastic season last year, Manchester United go into the new season with so much optimism they feel they can win everything and if they get the right formula, they can. Adding to the top quality team are players such as Jordi Cruyff and Karel Poborsky, who come to United with great Euro 96 performances behind them.
This year the squad is so strong and skilful that they are favourites for the League, and will go on to show the Continent that they are one of the best teams in Europe.

1 SCHMEICHEL

12 P. NEVILLE **4** MAY **5** PALLISTER **3** IRWIN

10 BECKHAM **16** KEANE

15 POBORSKY **11** GIGGS

14 CRUYFF **7** CANTONA

TEAM POSITIONS AND LINE-UP

1	Peter Schmeichel (GK)	15	Karel Poborsky
2	Gary Neville	16	Roy Keane
3	Denis Irwin	17	Raimond v/der Gouw
4	David May	18	Paul Scholes
6	Gary Pallister	19	Ronny Johnsen
7	Eric Cantona	20	Ole Gunnar Solskjaer
8	Nicky Butt	21	Patrick McGibbon
9	Andy Cole	22	Simon Davies
10	David Beckham	23	Ben Thornley
11	Ryan Giggs	24	John O'Kane
12	Philip Neville	25	Kevin Pilkington (GK)
13	Brian McClair	26	Chris Casper
14	Jordi Cruyff	27	Terry Cooke

Derek Whyte
Defender

Place of Birth   Glasgow, Scotland
Height   1.80m
Date of Birth   31-08-68
Weight   81kg

The Scotsman is now a major part of Bryan Robson's continental team, yet his job is to defend whereas the rest of them are happy to attack!

Having played over 200 games for Celtic, Derek moved a touch south to Teesside where he has become a firm favourite with the fans; he shows that resilience and determination are just as important as skill when holding your own in the Premiership.

The manager has frequently commented on how important Derek and the other British players are in Middlesbrough's revolution and their quest for the title.

Neil Cox
Defender

Place of Birth   Scunthorpe, England
Height   1.83m
Date of Birth   08-10-71
Weight   83kg

After helping the Riverside Stadium club to promotion, Neil has established himself in the Middlesbrough team and is without dispute their first-choice right-sided full back.

He has already proved his ability by teaming up superbly with Juninho in 95/96, and Bryan Robson will be hoping that the youngster, whom he signed from Aston Villa, can supply a hefty amount of crosses for new strikers Mikkel Beck and Fabrizio Ravanelli, making sure that 'Boro do not suffer the same second half of the season they experienced last year, and that they get a place in Europe.

Jan-Aage Fjortoft
Striker

Place of Birth   Aalesund, Norway
Height   1.90m
Date of Birth   10-01-67
Weight   84kg

Even though the arrival of mega-stars Ravanelli and Juninho has seen Jan's place in the team reduced, he is certainly not one to give up the fight for the striking role at Middlesbrough.

Having scored 28 goals for Swindon, and after a brilliant record of scoring a goal in every two games for Rapid Vienna before his spell in England, there were no doubts why Bryan Robson bought him in on a multi-million pound deal. Jan's time at Middlesbrough may be limited, but there is no doubt that he is a dangerous player who can torment defences with his strength and power.

Nick Barmby
Striker

Place of Birth	Hull, England
Height	1.70m
Date of Birth	11-02-74
Weight	72kg

After shining as part of Ossie Ardiles' 'famous five' for Tottenham, Nick became homesick so decided to move north to the Riverside stadium. He would hardly have believed then that he would soon be teaming up with Juninho, Emerson and Fabrizio Ravanelli.

Nick is not just concerned with Premiership football: Barmby was one of the good things to come out of the ill-fated England tour to the Far East prior to Euro 96, as he scored twice against China. Nick continued on form in the World Cup qualifier against Moldova, when he once again got his name on the score-sheet.

Fabrizio Ravanelli
Striker

Place of Birth	Perugia, Italy
Height	1.85m
Date of Birth	11-12-68
Weight	82kg

The 'White Feather' amazed everyone when he decided to desert the *Stadion Delli Alpi* and Juventus for the Riverside Stadium and Middlesbrough.

His goal in the Champions League Final will be remembered for a long time, and proved that he is a man of great skill, with a touch that belies his large physique.

He is also very strong in the air, and will undoubtedly be looking forward to teaming up with Juninho to bring some trophies back to the North East under Bryan Robson.

Juninho
Striker

Place of Birth	Sao Paulo, Brazil
Height	1.65m
Date of Birth	22-02-73
Weight	62kg

When this Brazilian came to England with his boyish looks and tiny frame, fans and footballers alike were unsure how he would perform, but he has proved himself beyond a measure of doubt.

The samba came to the Riverside with this colourful character, and Juninho's skill has seldom been seen in England; it has brought a whole new dimension to Middlesbrough's game.

Even with the arrival of more Brazilians and other international superstars, the £5 million signing is still in the limelight at 'Boro, and Juninho will be expected to make things tick.

Middlesbrough
STATS AND FACTS

Manager: Bryan Robson
Captain: Nigel Pearson
Colours: Home - Red and White
Away - White and Royal Blue
Ground: Riverside Stadium

CLUB HONOURS

None...so far!

TITLE ODDS
50/1
ON AUGUST 17th, START OF SEASON

What are their chances?

This season, Middlesbrough fans will see a team that three years ago they could have only dreamt about. World superstars such as Ravanelli, Juninho, Barmby and Emerson will grace the magnificent Riverside Stadium.

Bryan Robson is a manager with big ambition and big ideas, having spent £25 million on his squad this is the season that should change the Middlesbrough records and get something on the honours sheet. A possible cup victory and European place are what is expected from 'Boro this season.

Fabrizio Ravanelli

INS AND OUTS

INS	OUTS
Emerson **Porto**	Paul Wilkinson **Barnsley**
Fabrizio Ravanelli **Juventus**	Jamie Moreno **Washington DC Utd**
Mikkel Beck **Cologne**	

MILLER 1

WHYTE 3 · PEARSON 5 · VICKERS 4

COX 2 · FLEMING 14

MUSTOE 8 · EMERSON 6

JUNINHO 10 · BARMBY 7

RAVANELI 11

TEAM POSITIONS AND LINE–UP

(above)

INTERNATIONAL PLAYERS

Jan-Aage Fjortoft
Norway

•

Nicky Barmby
England

•

Juninho
Brazil

•

Fabrizio Ravanelli
Italy

•

Mikkel Beck
Denmark

1	Allan Miller (GK)	18 Graham Kavanagh
2	Neil Cox	19 John Hendrie
3	Derek Whyte	20 Philip Stamp
4	Steve Vickers	21 Craig Hignett
5	Nigel Pearson	22 Craig Liddle
6	Emerson	23 Jan-Aage Fjortoft
7	Nicky Barmby	24 Chris Freestone
8	Robbie Mustoe	25 Ben Roberts
9	Mikkel Beck	26 Chris Morris
10	Juninho	27 Michael Barron
11	Fabrizio Ravanelli	28 Viv Anderson
12	Alan Moore	29 Jamie Pollock
13	Gary Walsh (GK)	30 Branco
14	Curtis Fleming	31 Alan White
15	Phil Whelan	32 Andrew Campbell
16	Bryan Robson	33 Mark Summerbell
17	Clayton Blackmore	34 Keith O'Halloran

Keith Gillespie
Midfielder

Place of Birth	Larne, Ireland
Height	1.77m
Date of Birth	18-02-75
Weight	69kg

Keith must be one of the revelations of the Premiership. After breaking into the Manchester United first team, Keith found himself moving to St. James' Park in a deal which saw Andy Cole moving the other way for £6 million.

Even though Andy settled in quite well at Old Trafford, it is Keith who has exploded onto the scene, wearing the Newcastle shirt.

His pace and ability to whip in tantalising crosses have caused many Premiership defenders trouble.

A regular in both the Newcastle and Northern Ireland teams, he is certainly destined for the top.

Shaka Hislop
Goalkeeper

Place of Birth	London, England
Height	1.90m
Date of Birth	22-02-69
Weight	90kg

Newcastle United's keeper enjoys acting as a disc jockey as well as goalkeeping, but his priority lies with the team.

The London-born shot-stopper knows that if his form dips, then his starting place will go to Pavel Srnicek. That is as much motivation as he needs, and it has always been the youngster's aim to play in the top flight.

It surprised many when Kevin Keegan splashed out over £1 million to Reading for his services, but there is little doubt that his transfer fee would now be much greater.

Philippe Albert
Defender

Place of Birth	Buillon, Belgium
Height	1.90m
Date of Birth	10-08-67
Weight	90kg

Philippe is far from a typical 'English' style centre half. He has fantastic ability on the ball, is a good defender with the added bonus of strong attacking capabilities.

In the second half of the 95/96 campaign, Newcastle often had to rely on his goals as players like Ferdinand, Ginola and Beardsley found it increasingly difficult to score.

However, even though the signing of Alan Shearer has meant that Newcastle are more formidable than ever going forward, it has also meant that 'Super Kev' is inclined to play a more traditional back four, placing Howey and Peacock before Albert.

Kevin does know that Philippe will not be content to sit on the bench and will continue to fight for his place until he is established.

Les Ferdinand
Striker

Place of Birth   London, England
Height   1.80m
Date of Birth   18-12-66
Weight   85kg

Even though he scored more goals for Newcastle in the 1996 season than anyone since the days of Jackie Milburn, Les is always critical of his own game and never happy unless he is continuously getting the goals. Kevin Keegan has now created the most dazzling strike-force in the Premiership, with the talents of Les being combined with those of £15 million Alan Shearer and Faustino Asprilla. Les started the season superbly and will be on the shoulders of club team-mate, Alan Shearer, when it comes to selecting the front man for the national side.

Alan Shearer
Striker

Place of Birth   Newcastle-upon-Tyne, England
Height   1.80m
Date of Birth   13-08-70
Weight   79kg

Not a lot can be said about Alan Shearer after his £15 million move from former Premiership champions Blackburn Rovers to Newcastle United.

Being the world's most expensive signing, the striker has much to prove; yet his confidence is apparent and the man is the epitome of a great sportsman.

There is much speculation about who will partner Alan, but one thing is certain – Alan Shearer is a '30 goals a season man', and a wise investment at any price.

David Ginola
Striker

Place of Birth   Gassin, France
Height   1.83m
Date of Birth   25-01-67
Weight   74kg

Though reports may have indicated that David was unsettled at Newcastle, fans can rest assured that he is raring to go and ready to recapture last season's form. The stylish Frenchman has brought some class to the 'Magpies' and has a great rapport with the crowd. His tricks and ability to drift in and out of positions are fantastic! With Newcastle really pushing for the title this season, there is no one more determined than David to get a Championship medal in his cabinet.

STATS AND FACTS

CLUB HONOURS

LEAGUE
Champions:
1904–05, 1906–07, 1908–09, 1926–27

FA CUP
Winners:
1910, 1924, 1932, 1951, 1952, 1955

Manager: Kevin Keegan
Captain: Peter Beardsley
Colours:
Home - Black and White
Away - Blue
Ground: St James' Park

INS AND OUTS

Alan Shearer
Blackburn

What are their chances?

With the three-pronged attack of Asprilla, Ferdinand and record-buy, Alan Shearer – attacking-wise they are one of the most exciting teams in the world!

Kevin Keegan is now looking for rewards after spending £60 million at Newcastle. This season they need to avoid last season's problem of being too attack-minded and slapdash in defence. The arrival of Alan Shearer will either take a lot of pressure off other players and get the goals in, or create a detrimental amount of pressure to bring the trophies in and prove Alan's worth. Either way, a European place is likely.

Steve Howey

TITLE ODDS
2/1
ON AUGUST 17th, START OF SEASON

Keith Gillespie

Robert Lee

INTERNATIONAL PLAYERS

Pavel Srnicek
Czech Rep.

David Batty
England

Steve Howey
England

Alan Shearer
England

Les Ferdinand
England

Faustino Asprilla
Colombia

Keith Gillespie
N. Ireland

Philippe Albert
Belgium

TEAM POSITIONS AND LINE–UP

1	Pavel Srnicek (GK)	**17**	Jimmy Crawford
2	Warren Barton	**18**	Keith Gillespie
3	John Beresford	**19**	Steve Watson
4	David Batty	**20**	Lee Clark
5	Darren Peacock	**24**	Chris Holland
6	Steve Howey	**25**	Paul Brayson
7	Robert Lee	**26**	Robbie Ellliot
9	Peter Beardsley	**27**	Philippe Albert
10	Alan Shearer	**28**	Paul Kitson
11	Faustino Asprilla	**29**	Steve Harper (GK)
14	David Ginola		
15	Shaka Hislop (GK)		
16	Darren Huckerby		

Stuart Pearce
Defender

Place of Birth London, England
Height   1.78m
Date of Birth   24-04-62
Weight   82kg

'Psycho' is one of the great characters of the Premiership. His performances for England in Euro 96 were such that praise rang out from all corners of England and he was hailed a hero.

He is player with unquestionable drive, and one who gets his fair share of goals with his venomous left foot. At the age of 34, he may be considering that this season will be his last, but he will still play a vital role in Forest's Premiership progress.

Mark Crossley
Goalkeeper

Place of Birth Barnsley, England
Height   1.83m
Date of Birth   16-06-69
Weight   102kg

A product of the Forest youth team, Mark has grown into a capable and experienced keeper. The Forest faithful feel confident having the hands of six foot Mark in their goal.

After progressing through the ranks and learning from former keeper Steve Sutton, he now has over 230 appearances to his name.

It seemed his future was in doubt with a disputed contract agreement, but it was resolved and he hopes to bring Forest the glory they had in the Premiership 94/95 campaign.

Colin Cooper
Defender

Place of Birth Durham, England
Height   1.75m
Date of Birth   28-02-67
Weight   74kg

After his performance for England during the 1995 Umbro Cup it looked as though Colin's career could only go forward, but Nottingham Forest's dismal league performances in 95/96 saw Colin's form also suffer slightly. However, his skill kept the City Ground outfit away from the struggle of a relegation battle at the bottom of the Premiership.

Frank Clark snapped him up from Millwall where he learnt his trade. Colin has a strange ability for a centre back in that he is a very skilful free-kick taker, especially from long distances.

Ian Woan
Midfielder

Place of Birth   Wirral, England
Height   1.78m
Date of Birth   14-12-67
Weight   74kg

In one form or another, most of Ian's 95/96 campaign was surrounded by controversy.

It looked as though Ian would leave the club after his and the team's dismal showing against European opponents, Bayern Munich. Although he apparently settled any differences with Frank Clark, Ian was continually linked with a move to Tottenham, Everton or Leeds.

On the other hand, Ian enjoyed one of his best seasons at home. In a Forest team clearly affected by the loss of Collymore, Ian was their most consistent performer and most prolific goalscorer.

Perhaps the most crucial goal of the 95/96 season was scored by Ian against Newcastle at the City Ground.

The goal all but handed the Championship to Manchester United. Now, with the loss of Steve Stone for the whole of 96/97, there is even more pressure on Ian to produce the goods.

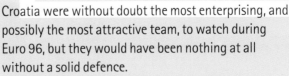

Dean Saunders
Striker

Place of Birth   Swansea, Wales
Height   1.73m
Date of Birth   21-06-64
Weight   66kg

'Deano' is the perfect example of a 'twenty goals a season man', and he has an amazing ability to score goals at whichever club he plays for, irrespective of the players around him. The world of football is unlucky that he may never grace the World Cup finals, especially if Wales fail to qualify for France in 1998.

He started his league life at Oxford before moving to Aston Villa and then to Liverpool. He followed former manager Graeme Souness to Galatasaray, where he became an instant hit, scoring the winning goal in the Cup Final against Fenerbahce.

Frank Clark and Dean will both be hoping that he continues to fire on all cylinders at the City Ground.

Nikola Jerkan
Defender

Place of Birth   Zagreb, Croatia
Height   1.83m
Date of Birth   18-12-64
Weight   84kg

Croatia were without doubt the most enterprising, and possibly the most attractive team, to watch during Euro 96, but they would have been nothing at all without a solid defence.

Everyone knew about Bilic and Stimac, but it was Nikola Jerkan who also stood out, especially thanks to his ability to run out of defence with the ball.

Nottingham Forest appear to have scooped a real bargain when they paid Spanish side Real Oviedo just over £1 million for his services, and he himself has made an attempt to hide his excitement about playing alongside new team mates such as Stuart Pearce and Dean Saunders.

Nottingham Forest

Nottingham Forest
STATS AND FACTS

Manager: Frank Clark
Captain: Stuart Pearce
Colours: Home - Red, White and Black
Away - Yellow and Navy Blue
Ground: City Ground

CLUB HONOURS

LEAGUE
Champions:
1977–78

FA CUP
Winners:
1898, 1959

LEAGUE CUP
Winners: 1978, 1979,
1989, 1990

EUROPEAN CUP
Winners: 1979, 1980

EUROPEAN SUPER CUP
Winners: 1980

What are their chances?

Nottingham Forest are a team that seems to be declining; stars are leaving and second-rate players are coming in. With Collymore gone and others set to follow, Forest do not seem able to recapture the form of two seasons ago which saw them reach third spot immediately after promotion.
Dean Saunders may be able to get his goalscoring touch back and, if he does, another European spot is within reach, but definitely no more than that.

INS AND OUTS

INS	OUTS
Dean Saunders **Galatasaray**	Kingsley Black **Grimsby**
Chris Allen **Oxford**	Neil Webb **Exeter**
Nikola Jerkan **Oviedo**	

INTERNATIONAL PLAYERS

(above)
Steve Stone
England

•

Stuart Pearce
England

•

Dean Saunders
Wales

•

Alan Fettis
N. Ireland

•

Nikola Jerkan
Croatia

•

(below)
Scott Gemmill
Scotland

TEAM POSITIONS AND LINE-UP

#	Player	#	Player
1	Mark Crossley (GK)	15	Andrea Silenzi
2	Des Lyttle	16	Nikola Jerkan
3	Stuart Pearce	17	Chris Allen
4	Colin Cooper	18	Alf-Inge Haaland
5	Steve Chettle	19	Stephen Howe
6	Chris Bart-Williams	20	Paul McGregor
7	David Phillips	21	Vance Warner
8	Scott Gemmill	22	Bryan Roy
9	Dean Saunders	23	Tommy Wright (GK)
10	Kevin Campbell	24	Richard Irving
11	Steve Stone	25	Steve Blatherwick
12	Jason Lee	26	Craig Armstrong
13	Alan Fettis (GK)	30	Richard Clark (GK)
14	Ian Woan		

Pitch diagram:

- 1 CROSSLEY
- 4 COOPER
- 5 CHETTLE
- 16 JERKAN
- 3 PEARCE
- 6 BART-WILLIAMS
- 14 WOAN
- 11 STONE
- 22 ROY
- 10 CAMPBELL
- 9 SAUNDERS

Kevin Pressman
Goalkeeper

Place of Birth	Fareham, England
Height	1.85m
Date of Birth	06-11-67
Weight	95kg

Kevin is an astute goalkeeper who has received criticism about some of his performances, but is now recognised as the number one keeper, although he had to battle for the goalkeeper's jersey with ex-England international, Chris Woods.

There was a stage three seasons ago, when Kevin was knocking on the door for an England call-up, yet he has had some problems since. Maybe this season he can recapture the form which everyone knows him to be capable of?

He is a strong and agile goalie whose ability has never been in doubt.

Des Walker
Defender

Place of Birth	Hackney, England
Height	1.80m
Date of Birth	26-11-65
Weight	75kg

Quiet man Des is still regarded as one of the top defenders in the country with his pace and precision, but Des has never seemed to play as well as he did when at Nottingham Forest. After an unsettled time in Sampdoria, and with his England career coming to a premature end, Des has recovered his form and can look forward to a possible place in the England squad. He has become a firm favourite with the crowd at Hillsborough and maybe this season will be the one when he scores that elusive first goal for the club.

Mark Pembridge
Midfielder

Place of Birth	Merthyr Tydfil, Wales
Height	1.70m
Date of Birth	29-11-70
Weight	75kg

After his very impressive first season in the Premiership, the Welsh international goes into this season hoping to build upon his solid reputation. Mark's aim has been to re-new the successful partnership he had with David Pleat at Luton. Mark is a talented, enthusiastic and determined player and, at the heart of the Wednesday midfield, he gives a very good balance to the side.

Reggi Blinker
Striker

Place of Birth	Surinam, Holland
Height	1.73m
Date of Birth	04-06-69
Weight	73kg

Another dread-locked Dutchman, Reggi is a player who has made an immediate impact on the Hillsborough crowd.

At £275,000, Reggi must surely be one of the bargain buys of all time. He proved right from the start that he was more than capable, with two fantastic goals against Aston Villa towards the end of the 95/96 season. David Pleat has stressed that Reggi is a major part of Sheffield Wednesday's new-look team, and hopes that along with the other major signings, Reggi can prove a significant success.

Chris Waddle
Striker

Place of Birth	Hedworth, England
Height	1.85m
Date of Birth	14-12-60
Weight	84 kg

Nicknamed the 'Wizard of Dribble', Chris has always been considered one of the most exciting players England has ever produced. He made his name at Newcastle, before being transferred to Tottenham Hotspur. He went on to win the European Cup with Marseille in France before returning to Sheffield Wednesday. Chris was instrumental in getting England to the 1990 World Cup Semi-Finals, despite his infamous penalty miss, and in 1993 he was named Footballer of the Year. Approaching the end of his career, he will surely be looking into either coaching or managerial positions.

David Hirst
Striker

Place of Birth	Barnsley, England
Height	1.83m
Date of Birth	07-12-67
Weight	86kg

David is one of the most talented strikers in the Premiership. However, he has never been able to fulfill that potential, largely because he rarely goes through a whole season without enduring some type of injury.

After a long and hard 95/96 campaign, David Pleat has made several changes, including the addition of the young and promising striker, Andy Booth. Andy is a very similar striker to David Hirst, and it is for this very reason that some believed the partnership would not work. However, Pleat sees Hirst as the perfect mentor for Booth and also hopes to take full advantage of that well-known recipe for success – a mixture of youth and experience.

Hirst will not only be striving to go through the 96/97 campaign injury-free, but also to notch up his best goalscoring tally for some time, and prove to his critics that he is not dead and buried.

Sheffield Wednesday

Sheffield Wednesday
STATS AND FACTS

CLUB HONOURS

LEAGUE
Champions:
1902–03, 1903–04,
1928–29, 1929–30

FA CUP
Winners:
1896, 1907, 1935

LEAGUE CUP
Winners: 1991

Manager: David Pleat
Captain: Peter Atherton
Colours: Home - Blue and White
Away - Green and White
Ground: Hillsborough

INS AND OUTS

INS	OUTS
Andy Booth **Huddersfield**	Marc Degryse **PSV Eindhoven**
Matt Clarke **Rotherham**	Darko Kovacevic **Real Sociedad**
Scott Oakes **Luton**	Chris Woods **Colorado Springs**
Wayne Collins **Crewe**	

What are their chances?

David Pleat has been heavily criticised for his decisions and was booed off at the end of last season, but he has spent his money wisely in the transfer market. Young striker, Andy Booth, came in for a large sum together with Scott Oakes. Players of calibre, such as Blinker, Newsome and Hirst are all capable of doing well.

Many have tipped Wednesday to struggle, but their home record will be okay and give them mid-table security.

TITLE ODDS
100/1
ON AUGUST 17th,
START OF SEASON

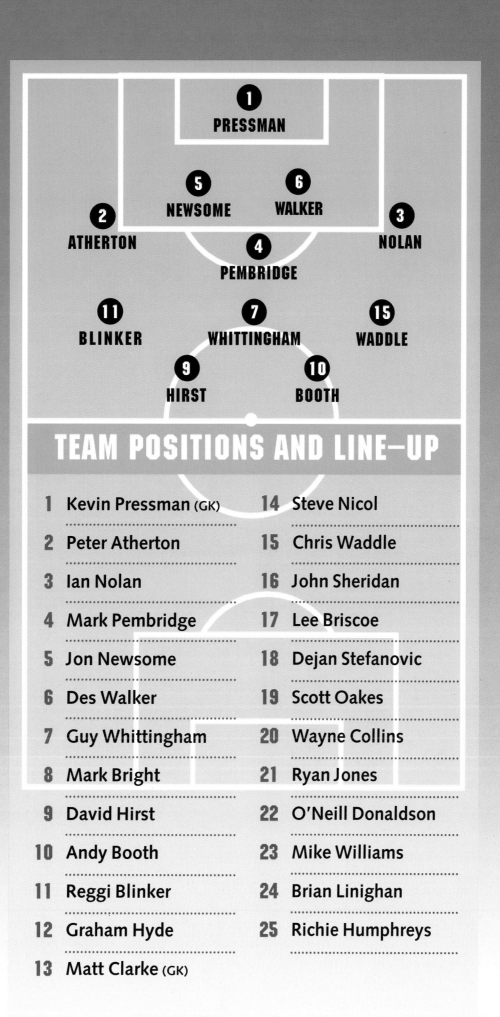

TEAM POSITIONS AND LINE-UP

1	Kevin Pressman (GK)	14	Steve Nicol
2	Peter Atherton	15	Chris Waddle
3	Ian Nolan	16	John Sheridan
4	Mark Pembridge	17	Lee Briscoe
5	Jon Newsome	18	Dejan Stefanovic
6	Des Walker	19	Scott Oakes
7	Guy Whittingham	20	Wayne Collins
8	Mark Bright	21	Ryan Jones
9	David Hirst	22	O'Neill Donaldson
10	Andy Booth	23	Mike Williams
11	Reggi Blinker	24	Brian Linighan
12	Graham Hyde	25	Richie Humphreys
13	Matt Clarke (GK)		

INTERNATIONAL PLAYERS

Mark Pembridge
Wales

■

Dejan Stefanovic
Yugoslavia

Ken Monkou
Defender

Place of Birth	Necare, Surinam
Height	1.90m
Date of Birth	29-11-64
Weight	91kg

The big, sturdy Dutchman has been a rock at the centre of Southampton's defence. His partnership with Richard Hall seemed one of the strongest in the Premiership; but now Hall has moved on, Monkou must find more to his game.

After his move from Chelsea four years ago, he has become a firm favourite with the Southampton crowd where his will to win and determination to keep the Saints in the Premiership have been his greatest asset.

The chance of forcing himself into the Dutch international team has now gone, but playing in the Premiership is a great achievement.

Jason Dodd
Defender

Place of Birth	Bath, England
Height	1.80m
Date of Birth	02-11-70
Weight	78kg

Behind Matt Le Tissier, Jason is the next Southampton player who scores great goals, especially from long distances. The fans at the Dell will tell anyone else that he is there primarily for his defending, and the goals are simply a bonus.

Graeme Souness will be hoping to continue Dave Merrington's good work and keep the young right back, who has everything a good full back needs. Jason's pace and passing ability mean that he could easily fit into the European style of play.

Graham Potter
Midfielder

Place of Birth	Solihull, England
Height	1.85m
Date of Birth	20-05-75
Weight	73kg

Graeme Souness' first summer purchase may not have been as immediately attractive as Ravanelli and Vialli, but there is no doubt among the 'Dell Men' that the newcomer will make as big an impact on the Premier League as at the club.

The 21 year old midfielder will relish teaming up with Jim Magilton, Neil Heaney and Matt Le Tissier in the Saints' midfield; and Graham's runs in front of the strikers make him very difficult for defenders to mark, and for other midfielders to track.

He moved from Stoke with the idea of Premiership football particularly in mind, and if anyone can help save the side from a relegation struggle it will be this tall midfield General.

Barry Venison
Midfielder

Place of Birth	Consett, England
Height	1.78m
Date of Birth	16-08-64
Weight	78kg

The flame-haired midfielder appears to follow or be followed by Graeme Souness, wherever they go. They started together at Liverpool, both soon moved to Galatasary and they now find themselves reunited at the Dell for a serious battle that neither have ever faced before – the fight against relegation.

Barry was rewarded early on in his Saints' career with the club captaincy, and his ability to motivate the team is second to none. He has a surprising amount of energy and is the perfect example of a box-to-box player, who runs huge distances during a game.

Jim Magilton
Midfielder

Place of Birth	Belfast, N Ireland
Height	1.85m
Date of Birth	06-05-69
Weight	90kg

The versatile midfielder has gradually established himself as the holding man in the Saints' midfield, while players like Mathew Le Tissier move further forward and endeavour to penetrate the opposition penalty box. However disciplined his defensive play, the experienced Saints' star does not mind moving forward and has managed to get his name on the team's score sheet on a number of occasions.

Graeme Souness will be desperate for Jim to keep getting the goals as Southampton strive to reach the safety of mid-table.

Matt Le Tissier
Striker

Place of Birth	Guernsey, Channel Islands
Height	1.85m
Date of Birth	14-10-68
Weight	86kg

Matt's skills, talent and potential are on a par with the very best players in the world. However, his performances for Southampton in the 95/96 campaign were anything but world-class. Matt failed to find the net half as many times as would have been expected, and performed well below his capabilities.

Throughout the season, Matt was linked with several top clubs in the hope of relaunching his career on both the club and international scene. Although he stayed loyal to the Dell, Matt continued to hinder his chances of making Terry Venables' squad with one bad performance after another.

The recent appointment of Glenn Hoddle to the England post has given Matt that extra bit of hope. Glenn is a publicly declared 'Matt Le Tissier fan', but Matt knows that he must improve his game and seize the opportunity when it arises if he wants to feature in the World Cup in France.

Southampton
STATS AND FACTS

Manager: **Graeme Souness**

Captain: **Barry Venison**

Colours: **Home - Red, White and Black**

Away - Yellow and Blue

Ground: **The Dell**

CLUB HONOURS

FA CUP
Winners: 1976

What are their chances?

After many seasons in the top flight, this year could see the end of all that for Southampton. Graeme Souness is a manager who has never experienced taking control of a struggling side.
Again, much will rely on Matt Le Tissier and if he doesn't perform they will find it difficult to score goals.
With Richard Hall gone, their defence seems much less resilient and this could prove a problem. Southampton are in for a tough time this season.

INS AND OUTS

INS	OUTS
Graham Potter **Stoke**	Richard Hall **West Ham**
Garry Monk **Torquay**	Tommy Widdrington **Grimsby**
Richard Dryden **Bristol City**	Mark Walters **Swindon**
	Bruce Grobbelaar **Plymouth**

Matthew Le Tissier

INTERNATIONAL PLAYERS

Jim Magilton
N. Ireland

■

Matt Le Tissier
England

TEAM POSITIONS AND LINE-UP

1	Dave Beasant (GK)	**13**	Neil Moss (GK)
2	Jason Dodd	**14**	Simon Charlton
3	Francis Benali	**15**	Alan Neilson
4	Jim Magilton	**16**	David Hughes
5	Barry Venison	**17**	Paul Tisdale
6	Ken Monkou	**18**	Matthew Oakley
7	Matt Le Tissier	**19**	Richard Dryden
8	Gordon Watson		
9	Neil Shipperley		
10	Neil Maddison		
11	Neil Heaney		
12	Graham Potter		

Barry Venison

Kevin Ball
Defender

Place of Birth	Hastings, England
Height	1.78m
Date of Birth	12-11-64
Weight	78kg

Another strong club man, Kevin shows the other players exactly what commitment is about, both on and off the pitch.

The man never gives less that 110%, and his heading abilities make the long ball tactic useless against the Sunderland defence in which he plays such a large part.

He signed from Portsmouth in 1990, and has remained at the centre of each Sunderland manager's plans since then. If he had reached the highest level sooner, international honours would surely have come.

Tony Coton
Goalkeeper

Place of Birth	Tamworth, England
Height	1.88m
Date of Birth	19-05-61
Weight	86kg

When Manchester United signed Tony Coton last season from neighbours Manchester City for a bargain £300,000, everyone knew his chances would be limited with the 'Great Dane', Peter, keeping goal.

Tony made his name with Watford, and from there he moved to Maine Road, and even received England recognition.

Tony has now teamed up with former team-mate, Peter Reid, to help Sunderland keep themselves in the Premiership.

Michael Gray
Stiker

Place of Birth	Sunderland, England
Height	1.73m
Date of Birth	03-08-74
Weight	67kg

The long-haired youngster has become a firm favourite with all of Sunderland's fans; both male and female drool over his every move, sometimes for different reasons!

He broke into the first team in 1992, and was quickly promoted to the England under-21 ranks. His performances as either left back or left winger, as well as his ability to cut inside and shoot viciously, have made him a target for all of the top clubs, but the Sunderland board have plastered a huge transfer fee on their new star.

Lee Howey
Striker

Place of Birth	Sunderland, England
Height	1.88m
Date of Birth	01-04-69
Weight	86kg

The only problem the Sunderland hero has is being placed in the shadow of his brother Steve, who has gone far with the England team thanks to his performances at Newcastle.

However, many say that Lee is the better player, with his versatility and height enabling him to perform commendably at both centre back and centre forward. This means that he is always guaranteed a place in the starting line-up whether he is stopping goals or scoring them.

Niall Quinn
Striker

Place of Birth	Dublin, Ireland
Height	1.93m
Date of Birth	06-10-66
Weight	100kg

Niall Quinn is a striker who is always willing to give 100% for his team and country. This has proved to be the main way he can sustain support from his fans.

Quinn's aerial ability is second to none (being taller than most of the other players it should be!), but for a big man, his touch on the ground is more than adequate.

A £1.2 million move back into the Premiership has given Niall a new lease of life joining up with old team-mate and manager, Peter Reid.

Alex Rae
Midfielder

Place of Birth	Glasgow, Scotland
Height	1.75m
Date of Birth	30-09-66
Weight	75kg

As the ex-Millwall man moves north, Peter Reid will be hoping to curb this midfielder's temper, encouraging him instead to concentrate on his attacking midfield skills. Alex has been booked and sent off a number of times, but this did not deter the Sunderland boss paying out over £1 million for the Scot who narrowly missed the Euro squad. The player fought hard to play in the Premiership in 1995, and his goals to games ratio is very impressive for a midfielder.

Sunderland

STATS AND FACTS

Manager: Peter Reid
Captain: Kevin Ball
Colours: Home - Red, White and Black
Away - White and Red
Ground: Roker Park

TITLE ODDS
250/1
ON AUGUST 17th,
START OF SEASON

What are their chances?

If there is any manager who is going to keep a team
in the Premiership through morale and determination,
then there is none better than Peter Reid.
Having worked wonders in bringing them up from the 1st Division
on very few resources, Peter will relish the challenge
of the Premiership.
Experienced players such as Stewart and Quinn will
prove vital for survival – a survival which is
well within their grasp.

CLUB HONOURS

LEAGUE
Champions:
1891-92, 1892-93,
1894-95, 1901-02,
1912-13,1935-36

FA CUP
Winners:
1937, 1973

INS AND OUTS

Alex Rae
Millwall

Tony Coton
Manchester United

Paul Stewart
Liverpool

Niall Quinn
Manchester City

Gordon Armstrong
Bury

Alec Chamberlain
Watford

72

Formation

```
                    1
                  COTON

            6           8
          MELVILLE     ORD
   2                              3
  KUBICKI                        SCOTT

            4           5
         BRACEWELL     BALL

  11                             7
 AGNEW                          GRAY

          10          17
        STEWART      QUINN
```

TEAM POSITIONS AND LINE-UP

1	Tony Coton (GK)	14	Lee Howey
2	Dariusz Kubicki	15	Alex Rae
3	Martin Scott	16	David Kelly
4	Paul Bracewell	17	Niall Quinn
5	Kevin Ball	18	Martin Smith
6	Andy Melville	19	Michael Bridges
7	Michael Gray	20	Darren Holloway
8	Richard Ord	21	Sam Aiston
10	Paul Stewart	22	John Mullin
11	Steve Agnew		
12	Gareth Hall		
13	David Pearce (GK)		

INTERNATIONAL PLAYERS

David Kelly
Eire

■

Dariusz Kubicki
Poland

■

Andy Melville
Wales

■

Niall Quinn
Eire

Niall Quinn

73

Gary Mabbutt
Defender

Place of Birth	Bristol, England
Height	1.75m
Date of Birth	23-08-61
Weight	80kg

When Gerry Francis came to Tottenham, the first problem he had to deal with was the weakness in defence. Many believed he would have to buy a top-quality centre half, but Gary Mabbutt ensured that Gerry did not have to spend a penny.

Rather than Gary's age being a hindrance, Gerry saw it as essential experience. 'Mabbs' has also been able to help youngsters come through the ranks and develop into top players, such as Sol Campbell.

It is therefore a credit to 'Mabbs' that Tottenham's defensive record in the 95/96 campaign was one of the top five in the Premiership.

There is no doubt that if Tottenham could, they would be relying on their inspirational skipper in the 96/97 season, but a broken leg on the opening game against Blackburn means they will have to do without him for some time, although he is sure to return to top flight action.

Ian Walker
Goalkeeper

Place of Birth	Watford, England
Height	1.85m
Date of Birth	31-10-71
Weight	80kg

Ian's recent form behind a vulnerable Tottenham defence has resulted in him being awarded his first international cap. Although he has no real chance at present of ousting David Seaman from the England number one position, Ian continues to establish himself as England's second-choice keeper. This is mainly because of his sharpness at crosses and his remarkable reflexes when it comes to stopping shots.

It has been a remarkable rise for a youngster who began his career on a Spurs youth training scheme.

Sol Campbell
Defender

Place of Birth	Newham, England
Height	1.85m
Date of Birth	18-09-74
Weight	89kg

Outstanding. This is the only word that can sum up the rise and rise of Sol Campbell. His versatility and strength are quite remarkable for such a young man.

He came through the ranks at Spurs and the youth policy developed his potential, surely setting him on course to be a future England centre back.

It was a major achievement to be included in the Euro 96 squad, and this taste of international competition will hold him in good stead for the coming season on both the domestic and international scene.

Darren Anderton

Midfielder

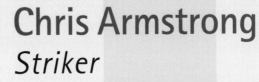

Place of Birth	Southampton, England
Height	1.85m
Date of Birth	03-03-72
Weight	76kg

The ex-Portsmouth starlet is slowly but surely recovering from the most serious injury of his career, and regaining the form that made him a regular in Terry Venables' England squads. The persistent and troublesome groin strain meant that Darren could only start eight games in the 95/96 season, but he was still fit for the European Championships.

Gerry Francis has interesting plans for the youngster, intending to move him gradually from the right wing to the centre of midfield, where he can be more involved in the game.

Chris Armstrong

Striker

Place of Birth	Newcastle-upon-Tyne, England
Height	1.83m
Date of Birth	19-06-71
Weight	84kg

Bought for £4.5 million, after his first ten games for Spurs, Chris did not seem threatening. Suddenly, he performed a dramatic turnabout – scoring 15 goals to great acclaim.

Chris' electric speed and strength in the air make him an ideal partner for Teddy Sheringham. The partnership has become feared throughout the Premiership, and Chris' reputation continues to grow. Much is expected of Chris this season, and he is tipped for England glory – following in the footsteps of his colleagues, Sheringham, Anderton, Campbell and Walker.

Teddy Sheringham

Striker

Place of Birth	Highams Park, England
Height	1.83m
Date of Birth	02-04-66
Weight	78kg

After an astonishing partnership with Klinsmann, Teddy showed his strength as a team player by forming a successful partnership with Chris Armstrong. Teddy had a great season both as a goalscorer and provider, and managed to convince many of his critics that he was worthy of his place in the England team.

And Teddy found no difficulty in linking up with any striker lined up with him by Terry Venables, so by the time the European Championships came around, he was in many ways regarded as the first-choice striker.

With Gary Mabbutt's sustained injury, Teddy is the replacement skipper for Tottenham. If Tottenham are to compete with the very best, Teddy will have to play the captain's role to the very best of his ability.

Tottenham Hotspur
STATS AND FACTS

Manager: **Gerry Francis**

Captain: **Gary Mabbutt**

Colours: **Home - White Blue and Yellow**

Away - Yellow and Blue

Ground: **White Hart Lane**

CLUB HONOURS

LEAGUE
Champions:
1950-51, 1960-61

FA CUP
Winners: 1901, 1921, 1961, 1962, 1967, 1981, 1982, 1991

LEAGUE CUP
Winners: 1971, 1973

EUROPEAN CUP WINNERS' CUP
Winners: 1963

UEFA CUP
Winners: 1972, 1984

What are their chances?

After a much improved season last year the future looks bright for Gerry Francis and his team.

Yet Gerry has not delved into the transfer market the way other Premiership managers have; he must feel as though his squad is good enough to challenge for major honours this season, without spending millions of pounds on transfer fees.

Much will rely on the form of Darren Anderton and Teddy Sheringham after impressive performances in Euro 96.

INS AND OUTS

INS	OUTS
Allan Nielsen **Brondby**	Chris Day **Crystal Palace**
Espen Boardsen **San Fransisco**	Steve Slade **QPR**
	Kevin Watson **Swindon**

INTERNATIONAL PLAYERS

Ian Walker
England

Colin Calderwood
Scotland

Sol Campbell
England

Allan Nielsen
Denmark

Darren Anderton
England

Ronnie Rosenthal
Israel

Teddy Sheringham
England

TEAM POSITIONS AND LINE-UP

1	Ian Walker (GK)	15	Clive Wilson
2	Dean Austin	16	Ronny Rosenthal
3	Justin Edinburgh	18	Gerald McMahon
4	David Howells	19	Kevin Scott
5	Colin Calderwood	21	Danny Hill
6	Gary Mabbutt	22	David Kerslake
7	Ruel Fox	23	Sol Campbell
9	Darren Anderton	24	Jason Cundy
10	Teddy Sheringham	25	Danny Carr
11	Chris Armstrong	26	Paul Maham
12	Jason Dozzell	27	Andy Sinton
13	Espen Baardsen (GK)	28	Allan Nielsen
14	Stuart Nethercott		

Julian Dicks
Defender

Place of Birth	Bristol, England
Height	1.78m
Date of Birth	08-08-68
Weight	83kg

Many have said that Julian is the hardest man in the Premier League, but he has calmed down after all his problems a couple of years ago. Harry Redknapp has rewarded Julian's change of attitude by making him captain. Julian was only booked twice in the latter half of the 95/96 season, and is adjusting quickly to his new position as the left-sided third of the new back three including Marc Rieper and Slaven Bilic.

After his dazzling displays in 1996, many found it astonishing that Terry Venables continued to ignore him and refused to select him for his Euro 96 squad. However, Julian has always stated that any international caps would be an absolute bonus.

Slaven Bilic
Defender

Place of Birth	Croatia
Height	1.88m
Date of Birth	11-09-68
Weight	85kg

'Super Slav' has immediately become a firm favourite with the Upton Park faithful. His determination, his will to win and his loyalty have made him a smash hit with the crowd.

Slaven signed in February '96 for the Hammers in a deal which, at the time, broke their transfer record at a cool £1.7 million. The cosmopolitan centre back is part of the growing number of Croatians joining Premiership clubs; he is a passionate player and has already made a major impact on his new club.

Ilie Dumitrescu
Midfielder

Place of Birth	Bucharest, Romania
Height	1.73m
Date of Birth	06-01-69
Weight	67kg

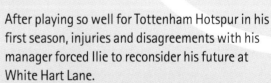

After playing so well for Tottenham Hotspur in his first season, injuries and disagreements with his manager forced Ilie to reconsider his future at White Hart Lane.

In December '95, the striker signed for West Ham in order to join their ever-growing European contingent. Yet he was not allowed to play due to the fact that he did not receive his work permit until March '96.

A very skillful player who is able to baffle defenders – West Ham will hope that Ilie shows the same determination as he did for Romania in the '94 World Cup.

Ian Bishop
Midfielder

Place of Birth   Liverpool, England
Height   1.75m
Date of Birth   29-05-65
Weight   69kg

'Bish' is one of the charismatic players of the Premiership, who sometimes fails to get the recognition he deserves. His tireless work in the middle of the park has helped West Ham's growth in the top league. His long hair, good looks, grace and flair make him a very distinguished player. He is adding more bite and strength to his passing, but with a limited number of centre midfield places available this season versus a wide spectrum of talented players, Ian will have to work much harder for his place this year.

Florin Raducioiu
Striker

Place of Birth   Bucharest, Romania
Height   1.79m
Date of Birth   17-03-70
Weight   72kg

The £2.4 million signing of Raducioiu broke West Ham's all-time record, and the 'super striker' has plenty to prove.

Even though he did manage to get on the score sheet once during Euro '96, he failed to show the West Ham fans his true potential. Injuries have halted his progress in the last year, but if he can deliver the form showed during the '94 World Cup, he will certainly have West Ham fans firmly on his side. His career has taken him all over the world: F.C. Porto, AC Milan and Espanol have all featured on Florin's list. Now, at 26-years-old, he is at the peak of his career.

Paulo Futre
Striker

Place of Birth   Montijo, Portugal
Height   1.73m
Date of Birth   28-02-66
Weight   72kg

When Harry Redknapp signed Futre on a free transfer, the Upton Park faithful were delighted. Before a dreadful season dogged by injuries in Milan, Paolo was recognised as one of the world's greatest strikers. Like so many foreign stars, Paolo was keen to play in the Premiership, so much so that he rejected moves to clubs Sampdoria and Parma in order to play for the ambitious Hammers. Futre is hoping to form a successful partnership with Raducioiu and re-capture the glory days of McAvennie and Cottee.

West Ham United

STATS AND FACTS

Manager: Harry Redknapp

Captain: Julian Dicks

Colours: Home - Claret, White and Blue

Away - Ecru and Navy Blue

Ground: Upton Park

What are their chances?

The 'Foreign Legion' are becoming stronger and stronger; with additions such as Paulo Futre and Florin Raducioiu they may well be able to turn a few heads this year. Harry Redknapp has two vital jobs – to find the right team to play and to try and get all his players communicating. If the Hammers can match their great football with results, then maybe a challenge for a European place is not out of reach.

CLUB HONOURS

FA CUP
Winners:
1964, 1975, 1980

EUROPEAN CUP WINNERS' CUP
Winners: 1965

INS AND OUTS

INS	OUTS
Florin Raducioiu **Espanol**	Mark Watson **Bournemouth**
Mark Bowen **Norwich**	Dale Gordon **Bournemouth**
Paulo Futre **Milan**	Alvin Martin **Leyton Orient**
Richard Hall **Southampton**	Les Sealey **Leyton Orient**
Michael Hughes **Strasbourg**	Malcolm McPherson **Brentford**
Steve Jones **Bournemouth**	

INTERNATIONAL PLAYERS

Marc Rieper
Denmark

■

Florin Raducioiu
Romania

■

Keith Rowland
N. Ireland

■

Iain Dowie
N. Ireland

■

Ilie Dumitrescu
Romania

■

Mark Bowen
Wales

■

Michael Hughes
N. Ireland

■

Slaven Bilic
Croatia

TEAM POSITIONS AND LINE-UP

1	Ludek Miklosko (GK)	15	Kenny Brown
2	Tim Breacker	16	Paulo Futre
3	Julian Dicks	17	Stan Lazaridis
4	Steve Potts	18	Ilie Dumitrescu
5	Richard Hall	19	Robbie Slater
6	Danny Williamson	20	Mark Bowen
7	Ian Bishop	22	Adrian Whitbread
8	Marc Rieper	23	Steve Jones
9	Tony Cottee	24	Michael Hughes
10	John Moncur	26	Frank Lampard
11	Florin Raducioiu	27	Rio Ferdinand
12	Keith Rowland (GK)	28	Slaven Bilic
14	Iain Dowie	30	Steve Mautone (GK)
		31	Neil Finn (GK)

Oyvind Leonhardsen
Midfielder

Place of Birth	Rosenberg, Norway
Height	1.78m
Date of Birth	17-08-70
Weight	71kg

After an extremely impressive 95/96 campaign, it looks like Joe Kinnear has pulled off another transfer coup. Oyvind is a 'busy' type of midfielder who often makes great runs going forward and consequently chips in with his fair share of goals. Oyvind and Robbie Earle combine to make a deadly duo, although they sometimes do not get enough credit for their attitude and ability.

Oyvind has attracted the attention of many top clubs, such as former champions Blackburn Rovers. However, Joe is reluctant to let yet another of his stars go because, with the gap widening due to the money involved, he has to rely on his own players for Premiership survival.

Ben Thatcher
Defender

Place of Birth	Swindon, England
Height	1.80m
Date of Birth	30-11-75
Weight	79kg

Ben broke into the side at the same time that the club moved to the New Den from Cold Blow Lane, and his market value immediately rocketed as Premiership managers saw that he was good going forward but, more importantly, that he could defend as well.

Joe Kinnear was the only manager to put his money where his mouth was, and the £1.75 million fee may well be considered a bargain in a few years' time, especially as Thatcher looks set to become a key figure in future England plans.

Vinnie Jones
Midfielder

Place of Birth	Watford, England
Height	1.83m
Date of Birth	05-01-65
Weight	75kg

One of the great characters of the game, Vinnie's long career may be coming to an end as those weary legs have battled in so many games.

The 'hard man' of English football has been the subject of controversy, whether it be on the pitch or off, yet he has always led his Wimbledon team with great passion.

Surrounded by hype, Vinny has had trouble gaining recognition for his achievements, yet his vicious shot, unbelievable throw-in and presence on the field make him a player worthy of his place in the Premiership.

Robbie Earle
Midfielder

Place of Birth	Newcastle-under-Lyme, England
Height	1.75m
Date of Birth	27-01-65
Weight	68kg

The stylish midfielder is surely the next star off the Wimbledon production line that Sam Hamman will be hoping to sell on for a hefty profit.

Robbie is a very solid midfielder, but is perhaps the most prolific goalscorer for his position in the League, guaranteeing 15 to 20 goals for the Dons every season. Even more surprising is that the majority of his goals come from his head via set pieces, which is the basis of many Wimbledon goals. Joe Kinnear will be hoping that Robbie's goals will give the Selhurst Park outfit the extra points they need to turn mid-table into European qualification.

Dean Holdsworth
Striker

Place of Birth	Walthamstow, England
Height	1.80m
Date of Birth	08-11-68
Weight	76kg

Dean has now been a Wimbledon player for some years and his consistent ratio of goals to games has helped to ensure their Premiership survival. While Dean has been loyal to his club, the attraction of moving to a bigger one, where honours are more likely, has often appealed to him.

Dean again ended up Wimbledon's top scorer in the 95/96 season and, with growing interest from West Ham and Everton, a move looked more than likely for the summer of 1996. However, no deal went through and he began the season still at Wimbledon.

Dean seems to be lacking the impetus that epitomises the 'Crazy Gang'. One just wonders how much longer Dean will remain?

Efan Ekoku
Striker

Place of Birth	Manchester, England
Height	1.85m
Date of Birth	08-06-67
Weight	76kg

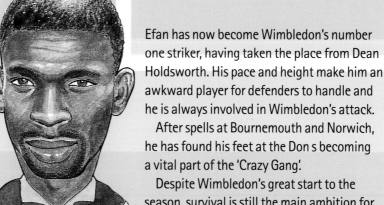

Efan has now become Wimbledon's number one striker, having taken the place from Dean Holdsworth. His pace and height make him an awkward player for defenders to handle and he is always involved in Wimbledon's attack.

After spells at Bournemouth and Norwich, he has found his feet at the Don s becoming a vital part of the 'Crazy Gang'.

Despite Wimbledon's great start to the season, survival is still the main ambition for the Dons, and Efans goals should ensure they stay up.

Wimbledon
STATS AND FACTS

Manager: Joe Kinnear

Captain: Vinnie Jones

Colours: Home - Navy Blue

Away - White and Black

Ground: Selhurst Park

CLUB HONOURS

FA CUP
Winners: 1988

TITLE ODDS
200/1
ON AUGUST 17th,
START OF SEASON

What are their chances?

Joe Kinnear and his side face a long, hard battle this season having spent very little money compared to their compatriots in the Premiership.
Ben Thatcher looks a good prospect, and the determination of Vinnie Jones and Robbie Earle will prove necessary if they are to survive.
The 'Crazy Gang' have had such an influence on the Premiership, proving a club can do well with few resources. But can they survive one more year?

Alan Kimble

Paul Heald

INS AND OUTS

INS	OUTS
Ben Thatcher **Millwall**	Steve Talboys **Watford**
Duncan Jupp **Fulham**	Leonard Piper **Gillingham**

Formation:
- 1 SULLIVAN
- 12 PERRY
- 17 MCALLISTER
- 2 CUNNINGHAM
- 6 THATCHER
- 7 LEONARDSEN
- 4 JONES
- 8 EARLE
- 11 GAYLE
- 9 EKOKU
- 10 HOLDSWORTH

TEAM POSITIONS AND LINE-UP

1	Neil Sullivan (GK)	14	John Goodman
2	Kenny Cunningham	15	Alan Reeves
3	Alan Kimble	16	Andy Thorn
4	Vinnie Jones	17	Brian McAllister
5	Dean Blackwell	18	Neil Ardley
6	Ben Thatcher	19	Stewart Casteldine
7	Oyvind Leonhardsen	20	Mick Harford
8	Robbie Earle	21	Duncan Jupp
9	Efan Ekoku	22	Andy Clarke
10	Dean Holdsworth	23	Jason Euell
11	Marcus Gayle	24	Peter Fear
12	Chris Perry	25	Andy Pearce
13	Paul Heald (GK)		

Oyvind Leonhardsen
Norway

Vinnie Jones

85

Fans opinions

Arsenal
James Browning, 13,
Finsbury Park

What do you hope for the new season?
I hope Arsenal can do well and win something in England.

What players are you most looking forward to seeing?
Of course, there's Bergkamp and Wright, but I've heard great things about the new French player, Christian Vieira and I hope he is the player we have needed for a long time!

Aston Villa
Paul Blenham, 14,
Birmingham

After a very impressive season last year, do you think they can improve?
Definitely. We have the best manager in the country and Sasa Curcic is the best midfielder, so we are all set to challenge for the title this year, even though we had a disappointing run in Europe.

Blackburn Rovers
Jamie Collins, 11,
Blackburn

Do you think Rovers can do well this year without super Alan Shearer?
I think that Ray Harford was daft to sell Shearer because he's the best player in the world, and he was the reason Blackburn scored all their goals. I don't think we have much chance of winning unless we buy good players to replace Alan Shearer.

What players would you like to see Blackburn buy?
Players who are nearly as good as Shearer: Roberto Baggio, George Weah and that Brazilian – Ronaldo.

Chelsea
Simon Laws, 12,
West London

Which of the new international players are you most looking forward to seeing?
I don't really know that much about Frank Leboeuf, but Roberto di Matteo looked good in Euro 96; and I think Gianluca Vialli has always been one of the most exciting players in the world.

Even though Chelsea now have a new manager, new players and ambitious directors, do you really think you have a chance of winning something?
Maybe not this year. But if we carry on buying top-quality players and keep Ruud as our manager we should win something soon.

Coventry City
Sivan Rubeet, 13,
Coventry

After last season's struggle against relegation do you think Coventry can finally give some happiness to their fans with the new faces who have been brought in?
Oh yes, Gary McAllister is one of the best midfielders in Europe, and with Eion Jess and Noel Whelan pushing forward, I feel Coventry can fight for a place in Europe.

Derby County
Jonathan Stammers, 11,
Derby

Finally Derby have gained promotion after spending many seasons trying to buy their way out of the 1st Division. Can they survive in the top flight?
Last season was the best I've ever seen at Derby, and with players like Dean Sturridge and Igor Stimac it proves that we've certainly got some players who'll contend with the likes of Shearer and Ferdinand.

What about the new signings of Christian Dailly and Aljosa Asanovic?
I don't know much about Dailly, but I saw Asanovic in the European Championships and it seemed that he is a skilful player and a cheap buy at £950,000.

Liverpool
Steven Graysfield, 12,
Liverpoool

With Manchester United and Newcastle spending large amounts of money and Liverpool not spending nearly as much, do you think it will give Liverpool less chance of winning the title ?
No, even though we have only bought Patrik Berger, I think we are strong all round from keeper to attack; and the arrival of Berger gives the extra option to play with more than two strikers.

But can you take the title from United?
I don't know. It is possible now they're in the Champions League – it may give us more of a chance.

Leeds United
Peter Lake, 10,
Leeds

As a young Leeds fan what do you think the new season holds in store for your club?
The players are really good. I love Tony Yeboah's brilliant goals and I've seen Lee Sharpe play for Manchester United – he will be very good for us. If none of our players get any injuries then maybe we can get close to winning the League.

Everton
Bobby Smith, 12,
Bootle

During the second half of last season Everton finished second best team behind Manchester United. Do you think they can carry this through to the beginning of the season?
We always seem to start slowly, but if we begin this season with fit players– especially a fit Duncan Ferguson – I think we can make a real impact.

Do you think Big Duncan is more trouble than he's worth?
No way! Behind Shearer he is probably the best striker in the Premiership . . . just watch out for him!

Leicester
Steven Franks, 11,
Leicester

Can Leicester do it? Can they stay up ?
Two years ago, when we were in the Premiership, it was a disastrous season: changing managers, a huge list of injuries and basically players who were not capable of competing with the big boys. Now we do have players who are good enough we could surprise a few people this year.

Manchester Utd
Gary Stapman, 12,
Manchester

It must be hard to see how Manchester United are going to be beaten this year, with all the talent and experience of last season and the wealth of exciting talent brought in this year? *Honestly, I think this year really will be the year for us. I think we can win everything there is to win with the squad we have.*

Everything? That is very optimistic. Don't you think that the players will get tired out by their European distractions? *Because of the size of our squad and the ability of it, I think we could pick two teams, each good enough to beat any team in our League.*

Sheffield Wed.
Terence Pilling, 12,
Sheffield

After a scare last season with relegation a close thing, how do you think the Wednesday players will respond as a new season begins? *The performances last season really made us Wednesday fans upset because we knew that we had a lot of really good players who just did not perform. This season I think we stand a good chance of winning a cup because the players will have had the pre-season to work together.*

How about the signing of Andy Booth? *I don't really know much about him but I've heard he is a young player with a lot of talent, which has to be good for us.*

Newcastle Utd
Joshua Bernstone, 11,
Newcastle

After last year's disappointment of losing the title, how do you think you will fare this year, especially with the signing of Alan Shearer? *Alan Shearer is the best striker in the world and I think he and Les Ferdinand will score lots of goals together. I still think Kevin Keegan is the best manager in the League, but he really needs to buy a defender because we have lots of players who like to score goals but not enough who can stop goals. I can't wait to see us play in Europe and I think we will definitely win the FA Cup.*

Middlesbrough
James Russell, 12,
Middlesbrough

As a team who were always known to be struggling and very unsure about their future in the top division, what do you think about the new wave of foreign talent? *I think it is brilliant. Juninho is one hell of a player – he probably has some of the best skill in the country.*

What about Emerson and Fabrizio Ravanelli? *I don't know much about Emerson, but I saw Ravanelli play for Juventus on television last year and he impressed me. I think we have a real chance of doing something this year.*

Nottingham Forest
Johnny Swales, 12,
Nottingham

Nottingham Forest are a team with a great deal of promise two seasons ago but now seem unable to recapture that form. What do you think about their chances this season? *We seem to be going through a lot of changes, what with Stan Collymore going and no one really capable of replacing him. Dean Saunders was brought in to score some goals, but I still don't think this will be a great season for Forest (compared to two seasons ago). But I do think we have a manager and a young squad who are capable of producing a really good team in the future.*

Southampton
Joanna Faye, 13,
Southampton

With most of the teams in the Premiership spending large amounts of money this summer except for Southampton and a few others, do you think this will give Southampton problems this season?
Yes, having only bought a few players from the lower divisions I think we will struggle to contend with the strength of the teams in the Premiership.

What about the arrival of Graeme Souness?
Honestly, I don't think it is a good move. He's a manager with a lot of determination but has never seemed to succeed in the jobs he's had in the past. Yet he might be just the man to get the best out of Matt Le Tissier and keep us up this year.

West Ham Utd
Nicholas Goldberg, 13,
London

After last season's solid performance in the Premiership and the arrival of many foreign stars, are West Ham destined for new heights?
Florin Raducioiu and Paulo Futre are two players I can't wait to see; Raducioiu is the striker we have been looking for to score at least 20 goals a season, and hopefully Futre will give us more magic than I have ever seen at West Ham.

So you feel confident about the new season?
Yes, very. I have never looked forward to a season more and I really feel we have a chance of winning something.

Tottenham Hotspur
Ben Tame, 12,
Tottenham

After seasons of inconsistency and near-misses for European places, how do you think you will fare this season compared to the other Premiership clubs?
The other teams in the Premiership have spent millions improving their squads, whereas we've only bought one unknown player. I trust Gerry Francis and the decisions he makes, but his lack of interest in the transfer market has made us Spurs fans wonder what he is doing.

And can you win anything?
I don't know. Maybe a good cup run and a European place, but I can't see us challenging for the title for a long time.

Sunderland
Scott Landon, 11,
Sunderland

After such a successful season last year do you think that Sunderland have a good enough team to stay in the Premiership?
Oh yeah! After last season we can only do well. We have the best manager in the League and so many good players that we will be able to beat the likes of Manchester United, Liverpool and Newcastle.

Wimbledon
Sam Robertson, 11,
South London

So, with the other big boys spending fortunes on international superstars and Wimbledon spending their money on young English talent in Ben Thatcher, do you think Joe Kinnear has made the right move?
I think the Crazy Gang can do it again because we've got Mick Harford and Vinnie Jones and they're strong enough for any opposition!!!???

Jody Morris
Chelsea

At only 17, this Chelsea youngster is already making a name for himself at Stamford Bridge. After one substitute appearance during the 95/96 season, Graham Rix has promised that we are bound to see a lot more of Jody this season.

He is a very gifted and talented player, who makes up for his lack of height in skill and determination. He is still at an age which calls for careful handling, but with such experienced players as Gullit, Vialli and Wise aiding him his future looks good.

Rio Ferdinand
West Ham United

Rio is one of the trend of top youngsters coming out of the West Ham youth policy. After top players such as Cottee, Ince, Potts

and, more recently, Williamson, Rio Ferdinand is next on the list.

The tall, slim central defender impressed many in his two substitute appearances for the Hammer's towards the end of the 95/96 season; he was called up to train with the full England squad in the Euro 96 build-up, and hopes to emulate the success of his cousin Les.

Michael Branch
Everton

Michael is very young, at 18, to have broken into the first team; but he is already starting to challenge strikers such as Paul Rideout and Graham Stuart for the place playing alongside Duncan Ferguson.

He matured last season after impressing in the reserves, and has given his all to the first team in the three matches he played. His speed and strength are astonishing and, with experience, he will aspire to be one of the Everton greats.

Michael Bridges
Sunderland

After really making a name for himself last season by scoring four vital goals in the push for promotion, Michael has already become a firm favourite with the fans.

The tall, yet pacey, striker has a real passion for the game and is a noticeably effortless worker. After going through the Sunderland youth ranks, he has now matured into becoming a top Premiership striker and Sunderland will have to work hard to keep him at Roker Park.

Emile Heskey
Leicester

At 18, Emile has already become a regular in the Leicester team and what a player he is! The tall, robust striker has electric pace and a great eye for goals. His name is on the tip of everybody's tongue and he is predicted to play a major role in helping Leicester survive in the Premiership.

At 6' 2" he is certainly not scared of anyone when it comes to strength, and his speed is such that it will scare the hell out of Premiership defenders. Leicester are going to have to offer Emile a good contract in the future if they want to keep hold of such promising talent.

Michael Owen
Liverpool

At only 16, Michael is already being put into the same category as Rush, Dalglish and Fowler, and to be compared to such prolific goal-scorers at such a young age really is an achievement.

In the 95/96 season, he broke schoolboy records by scoring an enormous amount of goals and landed himself Youth Player of the Year at Liverpool. He helped his team to win the FA Youth Cup and is tipped for great things in the future.

Managers

Arsene Wenger
Arsenal

Maybe it was fate that Arsene became manager of Arsenal simply by having the first five letters of the club's name in his!

Seriously, Arsene is one of the best managers in the world and has produced the goods wherever he has been in charge. His career really kicked off at Monaco where he managed to bring home the title and make Monaco one of the most prestigious clubs in French football. It was at Monaco that he first became acquainted with England by signing players, Mark Hateley and Glenn Hoddle. Arsene was then tempted away from French football by the glamour and money of Japan where he moved to Gary Lineker's former team, Grampus Eight. There he proved a success, but the challenge of Arsenal was irresistible. He is sure to rise to the massive task of resurrecting one of the great clubs of Europe.

Brian Little
Aston Villa

Having caused a storm when he dumped Leicester to return to the club where he made his name as a player, the Aston Villa manager has transformed people's views about him, with critics beginning to realise that he is a truly excellent manager.

Early signings of Mark Draper and Savo Milosevic may have surprised many, but Brian always knew what he was doing. The fact that Gareth Southgate is an England regular now he has reverted to a defensive role, is entirely thanks to his new manager.

A quiet man, he clearly likes to let his team's football do the talking.

Ray Harford
Blackburn Rovers

Having been right hand man to one of the most successful managers in Britain, Ray always had a tough job on his hands living up to his predecessor's reputation.

After previous management at Luton Town, where he took them to Wembley, Ray joined the staff at Blackburn. The rejuvenated side won their first League Championship in decades under Kenny Dalglish. It was always believed that Ray had played a major part in winning the title, yet when Dalglish decided to step down from managing, questions were raised about Harford's appointment.

After struggling to come to terms with Premier management at the start of the 95/96 season, Ray slowly progressed, improving his side to challenge for a UEFA cup slot.

Ruud Gullit
Chelsea

Dreadlocked and Dutch, the new Chelsea coach is untried at this level, but the Stamford Bridge faithful will be drooling over the football he is likely to provide, even if they are sad to see Glenn Hoddle go.

It is unlikely that stars like Leboeuf, Di Matteo and Vialli would ever have signed for the Blues if Gullit had not been manager, and his ideas, which have developed thanks to playing European football at all levels and in many countries, are bound to benefit Chelsea both at home and eventually abroad.

Arsenal

Aston Villa

Blackburn Rovers

Chelsea

Managers

Ron Atkinson
Coventry City

Big Ron is without doubt one of the most successful and charismatic managers of recent times.

He first made the headlines when he secured the FA Cup twice for Manchester United in the mid-eighties. He then moved to Sheffield Wednesday, where he gained promotion and beat his old club in the final of the League Cup. He also won the League Cup at Aston Villa, and guided the Villa Park side to UEFA Cup victory over Inter Milan.

Now at Coventry, he has teamed up with Gordon Strachan, and after two years of struggling, he appears to have built a squad capable of pushing for honours.

Jim Smith
Derby County

The 'Bald Eagle' captured everyone's heart when his young Portsmouth side lost on penalties to Liverpool in the FA Cup semi-final in 1992 after a brilliant cup run.

Jim always appears to be deep in thought, and Lionel Pickering and the Derby County board knew exactly what they were doing when they gave him the job of steering Derby towards promotion, because that is exactly what he has done.

He has proved to be a good judge of players by signing such stars as Stimac and Asanovic, BEFORE Euro 96, and before other managers got a chance to see them.

Joe Royle
Everton

An ex-Everton striker, he used to bang in so many goals that the Goodison Park crowd could not believe their luck. Since taking on a managerial role, his first task was to make sure that the club maintained their Premier League status, but he provided a bonus by bringing home the FA Cup and qualifying for Europe.

His reputation as a survivor began at Oldham, but he has nurtured players like Duncan Ferguson into promising players, and his signing of Gary Speed will boost the midfield.

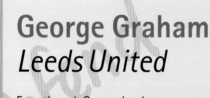

George Graham
Leeds United

Even though George has been surrounded by controversy over the past two years, the world of football has always known that he is a manager with exceptional confidence and ability.

As a player he was admired, and then his managerial career really kicked off at Arsenal where he won domestic trophies left right and centre and became the envy of every chairman.

But George left Arsenal under a cloud and an 18 month ban.

Now, on his return to the game, he is in hot demand, but it was Leeds that had the talent and lucrative deal to attract him; now he hopes to create a team to rival his quality days at Arsenal.

Managers

Coventry City

Derby County

Everton

Leeds United

Managers

Martin O'Neill
Leicester City

Over the last season, a cloud of controversy has surrounded the managerial career of Martin O'Neill, an honest manager who fully deserves the chance of having a go at Premiership football.

Martin became one of the most respected managers in football with the success he achieved at Wycombe Wanderers, bringing them from the Vauxhall Conference to the Second Division in three seasons. Under mounting speculation that he would leave, he eventually went to Norwich at the beginning of the 95/96 season but, after only six months, he moved to Leicester where he at first failed to deliver the goods. Then, in the last two months of the season, he took his team on a fantastic run and they won the play-off final against Crystal Palace.

Roy Evans
Liverpool

After such big name managers as Dalglish and Souness, Roy Evans was a surprise choice in Liverpool's search for success. However, Roy has been at Liverpool for many years, and was an original 'Shankly Boy'.

His work has often gone unnoticed, but now he is Liverpool's No.1 man; the team's progress must be attributed to him alone.

After a lack-lustre Liverpool team in the early '90s, Roy has carefully centred his team around a useful blend of youth and experience.

Alex Ferguson
Manchester United

Alex's arrival at any club seems to be a guaranteed signal for success. After great achievements in Scotland with Aberdeen, Manchester Utd decided that he was the man who would bring back the much needed, and much desired, silverware to the 'red devils' of Manchester.

Alex has responded in spectacular fashion, winning nearly every trophy possible, and recently became the first man to lead a side to two doubles. He is surely one of the greatest managers this country has ever seen.

Bryan Robson
Middlesbrough

'Captain Marvel' himself probably could not believe it when, in his first season in charge, he guided the Ayresome Park club to promotion to the Premier League. Since then, the club has moved to the Riverside Stadium, and Robson's signings of Juninho and Ravanelli have proved worthwhile.

He is now aiming to capitalise on his first season of Premiership management, as well as continue his influence in England's affairs, even though Glenn Hoddle has replaced Terry Venables in the top job.

Managers

Kevin Keegan
Newcastle United

Newcastle fans themselves know how one man turned a club from being on the verge of relegation to the old Third Division, into Premiership title-chasing contenders.

As one of the most inexperienced managers in the Premiership, his philosophical view of the game, and his fantastic support from both the fans and his board, make it easy to see why he has been such a success.

Already, Keegan has experienced European adventure, and the feeling of chasing a Championship. He showed great ambition with some expensive purchases – Les Ferdinand, Faustino Asprilla and David Batty, to name but a few.

Frank Clark
Nottingham Forest

He may appear to be quiet and shy on the outside, but his will to win is as strong as any other manager in the Premier League. When Brian Clough decided to retire, the then Leyton Orient manager was a surprise choice as new boss at the City Ground, but he immediately delivered promotion back to the top flight.

Early on, he had to overcome Stan Collymore's departure, but he did this easily with the arrival of established talent, for example Silenzi, Campbell, Jason Lee and, in the summer of 1996, Dean Saunders from Galatasary.

David Pleat
Sheffield Wednesday

David's football knowledge is recognised throughout the game. It is indeed this quality which has enabled him to succeed at a lower level with Luton Town, as well as enjoying a short spell at Tottenham Hotspur.

David was recently appointed as the replacement for Trevor Francis and, even though his first season was far from stimulating and his foreign imports far from impressive, David is in the process of 'rebuilding' and the Hillsborough faithful can rest assured that they are in stable and secure hands.

Graeme Souness
Southampton

With a return to Premiership management always on the cards, it has proved to be a somewhat turbulent ride for Graeme in his managerial career.

After stepping into the shoes of Kenny Dalglish at Liverpool, much was expected of Graeme, yet he failed to deliver and left under a cloud.

Graeme then took a rest from football, until he was given the challenge of taking the reigns of Turkish giants, Galatasary. The pressure eventually became too great, and he returned to England where he was snapped up by Southampton to replace Dave Merrington.

Newcastle United

Nottingham Forest

Sheffield Wednesday

Southampton

Managers

Peter Reid
Sunderland

Even though Peter suffered an unfortunate spell at Manchester City, his qualities as a manager have never been doubted. Sunderland realised this and turned Manchester's loss into their gain.

When Peter arrived, Sunderland were at the wrong end of the division. His principal aim at that point was survival. Not only did he achieve that aim but, within a year, he had transformed his team into a championship winning side.

Sunderland supporters believe that they are now in the division where they belong, and with a manager like Peter Reid, they can only achieve more success.

Gerry Francis
Tottenham Hotspur

Gerry possesses a ruthless style of management which has been an essential asset throughout his career.

He managed his beloved Q.P.R. for a number of years, where he transformed a money-stricken club into a relatively successful team. His ability to purchase players from the lower divisions, and develop them into top class internationals – for example Les Ferdinand – convinced Alan Sugar that Gerry was his man.

As yet, Gerry has brought no silverware to Tottenham Hotspur, but it is surely only a matter of time.

Harry Redknapp
West Ham

Harry is a manager who certainly knows the ups and downs of football management. After building his managing reputation with Bournemouth, he joined Billy Bonds at West Ham in 1991.

When the Hammers gained promotion in 1993 to the Premiership, Harry took full control of management at Upton Park. His first two seasons were mainly spent fighting relegation, but the 95/96 season proved to be a success seeing West Ham finish in 10th place.

Harry's ambition to continue the success in 96/97 is shown with the summer's major signings of Paulo Futre, Richard Hall and Florin Raducioiu.

Joe Kinnear
Wimbledon

Wimbledon's lack of resources make them a tip for relegation nearly every year, but, as Joe often points out, not only do they continue to survive, but they frequently finish in the top half of the table.

Joe manages to achieve this through 'bargain buys' and training his team to concentrate on their strengths.

Like his chairman, Sam Hammam, Joe is not frightened to voice his opinion in public and, as a result, often finds himself banished to the stands.

Review of 1995/96 season

The 1995/96 season will be remembered for a long time: thrills, upsets, great players and great characters all combined to create the most exciting season ever.

In the summer of '95 the transfer market was crazy; record-breaking deals were struck, while top international players arrived from all over the world: Stan Collymore moved from Nottingham Forest to Liverpool for an unprecedented £8.5 million; Les Ferdinand moved to Newcastle for £6 million and Chris Armstrong to Tottenham Hotspur for £4.5 million. International stars such as Dennis Bergkamp, David Ginola, Ruud Gullit and Savo Milosevic joined what was going to be the best league in the world.

The season kicked off with great anticipation; every club felt they had a chance of achieving something. Newcastle started brightest of all with their flair, and their attacking players – whether it be Albert, Ginola, Gillespie, Beardsley or Ferdinand – they just seemed to bamboozle every opposing team. Other players who surpassed themselves at their new clubs were Barmby at Middlesbrough, Kanchelskis at Everton and the wonderfully talented Dutch master, Ruud Gullit at Chelsea.

While Newcastle, Arsenal and, surprisingly, Aston Villa got off to fliers, favourites Manchester United and former Premier champions Blackburn Rovers did not quite hit the mark, yet Alan Shearer still managed to find the net regularly for a very average side.

The season continued with Newcastle leading the way and the Toon Army celebrating every weekend. At the other end of the table, it was looking ominous for Bolton Wanderers who never seemed to get a consistent team going and had managerial problems.

Other teams impressed – such as Tottenham Hotspur with their deadly strike force of Sheringham and Armstrong, yet their poor home record always seemed to let them down. After being tipped as relegation certainties, Harry Redknapp and West Ham proved everyone wrong by putting in some great performances and finding a jewel of a player in young Danny Williamson.

By January, Newcastle had a 12-point lead over a very young, but still enthusiastic, Manchester United team and at one stage bookmakers stopped taking bets on the Magpies to take the Premiership. Then it all seemed to go horribly wrong for Kevin Keegan and his team. While Manchester United found a winning formula by mixing experienced players such as Schmeichel, Bruce, Pallister and Cantona with fresh faces such as the Neville brothers, Beckham and Scholes, Newcastle's season started to go downhill. Much was blamed on the talented Colombian newcomer Faustino Asprilla for 'not being able to fit in'.

At the bottom of the table the furious fight against relegation hotted up. With Bolton never really having a chance of escaping the deadly relegation zone, it was a battle between Southampton, Manchester City, Wimbledon, QPR, Coventry and Sheffield Wednesday to see who would avoid the drop.

Despite a late flurry, the ever enthusiastic Ray Wilkins and his team were relegated along with Manchester City; they simply did not score enough goals – 33 in total.

Aston Villa impressed many with outstanding performances from players such as Gareth Southgate and Dwight Yorke; Brian Little and his side thoroughly deserved their place in Europe. Even though Arsenal could never recapture their early-season form, deadly Dennis Bergkamp helped them to a respectable season by gaining the final European place.

The race for the title was hotting up with Manchester United on devastating form – only losing one of their final sixteen games. However, Newcastle's form was inconsistent with cracks appearing in their defence, an area never really concentrated on by Kevin Keegan. It was on April 3rd that an epic game was played in which Newcastle lost the lead three times, eventually losing the title to Liverpool at 4 goals to 3 . . . you could see their luck was not in.

As for the champions? Well, they were criticised and derided, but Alex Ferguson proved everyone wrong by taking yet another Premiership title and putting himself in the record books by taking his team to a double double – winning the Premiership title and the FA Cup for the second time in three years.

Euro 96 Review – Football Came Home

What a Championship, what excitement, what atmosphere! In June 1996 football came home to England.

After weeks of build-up and press hype, England kicked-off the first major Championship to be held in Britain for 30 years. The atmosphere at Wembley was electric, the fans full of anticipation and hope that their country could produce something special. The first match was a disappointment with Switzerland surprising everyone with their slick style of play and managing to force a draw (yet failing to get another point in their other two games).

The group stage saw many teams struggle to cope with the intensity of so many games in such a short space of time; Italy, Romania and Holland fell victim to this. Italy were the major disappointment in the Championship, bowing out at the group stage and posing a question mark over the manager, Arrigo Sacchi, and his team selection. Romania did not impress many, their team looked old and weary with very little sparkle; they were the only team to fail to get a single point. Holland qualified, but their performances were never genuinely impressive and they seemed to lack the killer instinct that they have had for so many years.

Denmark, Switzerland and Bulgaria were never really expected to produce much , and therefore no one really noticed their failure to qualify for the quarter-finals. Yet performances from players such as Hristo Stoichkov, Brian Laudrup and Kubilay Turkyilmaz showed that these countries have potential.

Scotland were always ranked as outsiders and were never given a hope to even get a point. However, Craig Brown and his side made a real name for themselves in Euro 96 with strong, gritty performances. Hendry, McAllister and McCall were the engine that powered the rest of the team. A dogged performance against the Dutch gained a 0-0 draw, but they were unlucky not to get any points against rivals England, where Gary McAllister missed a penalty. A nailbiting finish to their Championship saw them beat the Swiss, but still fail to qualify for the play-offs by just one goal.

Then there were the nations that did impress and made Euro 96 the exhilarating three weeks it was. Portugal and Croatia were two inspirational teams at the group stage, yet could not muster the resilience to progress beyond the quarter-finals.

Players such as Costa and Pinto for Portugal, and Suker and Bilic for Croatia impressed and served warning that these teams certainly should not be underestimated.

France and Spain found themselves in the same group and showed they had a similar way of breaking teams down. They both came into the Championship with very strong reputations and lived up to them. The Spanish were somewhat lightweight in front of goal, but showed a good mixture of strength and skill in their build-up play, whilst the French were probably the best all-round team in the Championship, but seemed to lack that extra bit of passion and desire.

After a gruelling ordeal in the quarter-finals with players from all teams looking very weary, the selection was down to the final four: Germany, England, France and The Czech Republic. The Czech Republic had made it to the quarter final through sheer hard work and team spirit, and had become a popular team. Players such as Berger, Poborsky and Nedved proved that hard work and a will to win could give any team of superstars a run for their money – as the French found out – losing a semi-final penalty shoot out to the Czechs.

The tension was tangible as Terry Venables walked out with his England team to face his biggest ever game, against a German team that looked strong but not as determined as previous teams. The England team had brought so much joy to the country over those three weeks – but this was the one that mattered. Alan Shearer had become a hero, along with many others, and it was he who gave England an early lead, until the Germans quickly equalised with a neat Kuntz goal. So many near misses, so many 'oohs' and 'ahhs', it was one of Wembley's finest matches. It came down to penalties and David Seaman could not perform the penalty-saving heroics that he had performed all tournament long; it was the unfortunate Gareth Southgate who was the unlucky one whose penalty was saved and England were out of Euro 96.

The final was an anti-climax after this, but it was still an interesting contest. The Czech Republic were never expected to get past the group stage so to see them in the final was something that their fans had only dreamt of. They were even a goal up until late into the second half when an equaliser by super-sub Olivier Bierhoff saw Germany draw level. It was Bierhoff who scored the winner with the 'Golden Goal' rule, and Germany won their third European Championships.

England's recent level of play has won the heart of a nation, which has been deprived of footballing glory for so many years. England are now poised to make an impact on the world footballing scene. Terry Venables leaves Glenn Hoddle with a team that works well as a unit and is starting to look like a class act. The European Championships gave England the chance to show their ability, and performances against Holland and Germany in particular leave no doubt that we do have the talent.

Glenn Hoddle begins a new era and a new way forward, but one thing is certain – English football is on the way up.

Steve McManaman

Surely one of the 'unlikely lads' of Euro 96, Steve showed his abilities to the rest of the world, and earned himself a place in the recent poll of the world's Top Ten Players.

For those who have seen Steve play over the past four years, his ability was never in doubt; it's his consistency that has always had the question mark hanging over it.

At 24 years of age, his talents are very important to the future of English football and, with time, he will probably go down as one of the all-time greats.

Stuart Pearce

Stuart Pearce will go down with Alan Shearer and David Seaman as one of the great heroes of Euro 96. His bravery, enthusiasm and determination were why England did so well.

His penalty against Spain in the quarter-finals really underlined the courage of this man: after missing a vital penalty in the World Cup six years ago, he scored a perfect penalty in the Euro 96 competition. It is to Glenn Hoddle's relief that he managed to persuade Stuart not to retire from international football.

Paul Gascoigne

Question - *What would the England team be without Paul Gascoigne?*

Answer - *A lot more boring!*

Before the 96 Championships, controversy surrounded Paul after the episode concerning his night out on tour was made public. In fact, some demanded he be thrown out of the England squad. These people must know little about football as Paul proved once again during the tournament that he ranks alongside some of the best players in the world, and England need him.

He played more consistently than he has for a long time, but with his usual flair. There were several memorable moments of inspiration from the star, none more so than his magical goal against Scotland. At last Paul seems to have fully matured on the field, and he can now help other youngsters progress into what he is now - a star!

Alan Shearer

The Newcastle striker has undoubtedly put himself alongside the star forwards of Europe. There were many doubts hanging over his head after his mammoth goal drought prior to Euro 96, but he managed to silence the critics in the best possible fashion.

Alan scored goals against Switzerland, Scotland, a brace against Holland and an early strike against Germany; the months after saw a number of clubs falling over each other in a bid to get his signature.

Newcastle were the lucky ones, but England manager, Glenn Hoddle, will be hoping Alan can fire the national side into the 1998 World Cup finals in France.

European Players

GERMANY

With such dominant displays in Euro 96, the power team showed once again they are the greatest force in European football. Berti Vogts has made a team with all-round ability; with so much talent available to him, it is his true managerial skills that have shone during his time as German manager.

Young players such as Ziege and Bierhoff did their bit, but it was the coolness and level-headedness of Sammer, Hassler and Klinsmann which were so important to the Germans. With such a circuit of youngsters coming through, another trophy-taking team is in the making, allowing the Germans just to keep on winning.

Mathias Sammer

Few will argue with the fact that the Borussia Dortmund sweeper was the star player in Euro 96. Glenn Hoddle will spend many nights dreaming of producing a member of the back line who is just as accomplished and composed when he enters the opponent's half of the pitch.

Sammer scored goals against both Russia and the Czech Republic in Euro 96, and it is interesting to note that both goals came from open play.

Germany also had one of the best defensive records in Euro 96, showing that even though Sammer wanders forward, he never shirks his defensive responsibilities, and is always there to sweep up any dangerous attacks from the opposition.

Thomas Hassler

At 30 years of age, Thomas still plays a major role in the German team, adding that bit of flair to the strength and solidity of the team.

He was always a threat in Euro 96, and he played a major part in helping them to European success. His international career has glittered, having participated in German Championships in 1990/92/94 and 96.

GERMANY

Jurgen Klinsmann

At the age of 33, Jurgen is still considered one of the top strikers in the world; his finishing is second to none together with his powerful aggression.

His Euro 96 performance was exceptional – even after suffering an injury he came into the side scoring three great goals and helping Germany to another Championship. His brilliance could only have been expected in the light of his performances for Tottenham Hotspur and the name he has made for himself in England.

As he comes towards the end of his international career, it would come as no surprise to anyone if Jurgen one day takes over from Berti Vogts to become manager of Germany.

Andy Moller

Andy Moller has risen to the challenge of being the linchpin of the German side, and takes it all completely in his stride.

The forward going midfielder played a major part in Germany's success in Euro 96 by scoring and creating goals, yet his greatest moment of glory came with his winning penalty against England in the semi-final.

At the age of 30, the next World Cup will see an end to his international career, but his performances for Germany over the years will deservedly be remembered for a long time.

The Italians were a huge disappointment in Euro 96, and drastic change is needed in their game.

Surprisingly, Arrigo Sacchi kept his job after the Italians exited in the group stages of Euro 96. He must now realise the need to find a settled team from the amount of talented players available to him. They do have some of the finest calibre players in the world – for example, Maldini, Zola, Albertini and Ravanelli; and there are players who are both young and experienced, such as Del Piero and Chiesa. This bedrock of talent holds them in good stead, and with the right direction, they will be a force in the future.

Paulo Maldini

The long-haired darling of Italian football is now widely regarded as the best defender in the world, as well as being the first name on the Azurri team sheet. Performances for AC Milan have re-affirmed his reputation, but his performances in USA 94 were instrumental in his side's passage to the final. In Euro 96, he suffered from a troublesome leg injury, and could do nothing to halt his country's early exit from the competition.

Paulo is still young, and will undoubtedly help steer Italy to success in France 98, possibly as the captain.

Pierluigi Casiraghi

A surprise inclusion in the Italian squad over such superstars as Vialli, Baggio and Signori; the Lazio striker confirmed the Italian manager's confidence in him by notching up two goals in Italy's most impressive performance of the tournament against Russia.

Casiraghi will unfortunately be remembered for missing a glaring opportunity in the dying moments against Germany, which could well have seen Italy progress further.

Gianfranco Zola

The little terrier in the Italian midfield works ferociously to create chances and dazzle the opposition with his slick trickery.

Gianfranco was an important part of the Italian team – with no Roberto Baggio, it was up to him to produce the skill and ideas for Italy's attacking play. He was probably the most outstanding player in an Italian team that lacked confidence.

'Franco' will continue to work his hardest to get into the Italian team, but realises that the players he has helped come through – such as Alessandro Del Piero – could well be taking his place in days to come.

The French had the chance to show the rest of Europe what all the talk was about when they came to the European Championships. However, although there were great touches and flashes of inspiration, they never really fulfilled their reputation.

Many had tipped them to win the Championships, but with the controversy surrounding the French coach's decision to omit Cantona and Ginola, their task was made harder. Yet players like Djorkaeff, Karembeu and Blanc proved worthy of the praise they received.

Coach Aime Jacquet has done a superb job in turning an ordinary French team into one that was a strong contender at the Championships, and if they continue in the same vein they are certain to do well when the World Cup 98 comes around on home soil.

Christian Karambeu

Leading up to the Championships, France's record was surprisingly more impressive than any other country in Europe, if not the world.

The French coach established a hard-working and committed squad at the expense of the flair and charisma normally demonstrated by the brilliant Cantona and Ginola, who were both omitted from the country's Euro 96 squad.

However, Christian is the exception who fits nicely into both categories and consequently played an important role in France's progress to the semi-finals. He is still very young and is sure to feature in many future French midfields.

Didier Deschamps

The tiny midfielder really stamped his mark on world football throughout Juventus' victorious Champions League campaign of 95/96, when his ability to block other players, particularly Edgar Davids of Ajax in the final, allowed the front players to relax and perform to the best of their abilities.

In Euro 96, Didier was rewarded with the captaincy by Aime Jacquet, and he proceeded to bring honour to his country by steering them all the way to the semi-finals, even without David Ginola and Eric Cantona.

It was only the lottery of the penalty shoot-out that stopped him leading his side out in the final at Wembley.

Jouri Djorkaeff

Pretty much unheard of before the European Championships, he showed the rest of Europe what he could do with some sparkling performances, and featured heavily in nearly every French attack. His speed and agility tormented defenders and always gave the French an attacking option.

At 28, Jouri appears to be at the peak of his career and is all set to continue the progression of French football.

As victors of the European Championships two years ago, much was expected of Holland this time around, but it was never really meant to be.

The squad looked old and, with quality players such as Edgar Davids being sent home after the first game, the coach was obviously not on the same wavelength as many of his players. The only highlight of their Championships was a notable performance against the Swiss.

Guus Hiddink has taken on board the Ajax training method, basing his team around the Amsterdam club; is this a mistake that should be rectified? Holland is a nation of talented players such as the de Boer brothers, Kluivert and Bergkamp, so with stronger guidance in the right direction, they could succeed once again.

Jordi Cruyff

Jordis performance in England proved that he deserved his place in the side, and that Guus Hiddink had his team plan in order.

After a slow start against Scotland, Jordi found his form against the Swiss, running them ragged, and scoring a 20-yard goal for his side. In the quarter-finals, he was the only player who ever looked likely to threaten the French defence, and his team's defeat could not be blamed on him.

Now playing for Manchester Utd, he will be hoping to add significantly to his collection of caps.

Patrick Kluivert

Patrick is one of the hottest new names in world football. He is yet another youngster pushed through the Dutch ranks at Ajax.

After scoring the important goals against the Republic of Ireland that sent Holland into the European Championships, Kluivert did not feature much in the actual tournament. However, on the occasions that he came on as a substitute, he provided his country with much needed fire-power, as demonstrated against England at Wembley when he scored Holland's only goal which put them into the quarter-final.

Frank de Boer

At the age of 26, Frank and his twin brother Ronald have become legends in Dutch football.

Frank is a strong player who can play right throughout the team, and is a linchpin in both Holland's and Ajax's future success.

Frank's footballing ambition is 'to win everything at least once'.

European Players

Coach Javier Clemente came into the Championships with a strong reputation and conviction that the team would finally deliver in a major competition; a belief that was not fulfilled.

The team actually seemed to get stage fright at this major competition, and players who were expected to shine, simply did not. There were those who made a name for themselves, such as the pacey wing back, Sergi, and tough-tackling defenders, Alkorta and Nadal.

The Spanish team has great potential and, with a successful World Cup qualifying campaign, it is conceivable that they could go on to do great things in France, especially if players like Hierro and Caminero start to perform.

Miguel Angel Nadal

'The Beast' is a monster of a player at the heart of the Spanish defence. He is a very talented footballer with a sweet touch and strong presence.

He was sorely missed by the Spanish in their opening game, but went on to be a major part of their plans helping them to improve their standard of play and become more dominant on the field.

At the age of 30, Miguel is still regarded as one of the top defenders in the world, and after such an impressive Euro 96, he is being tempted by other clubs around Europe, including Manchester United.

Luis Enrique

Enrique is certainly one of the most talented players the Spanish have seen for a long time, yet he failed to deliver in both the World Cup 94, and in Euro 96.

It appears that he simply cannot recapture the form that he showed at Real Madrid, when he helped them win the title two seasons ago.

He will keep trying to get back into the national squad, especially now he has joined Bobby Robson's Barcelona in a multi-million pound deal.

Fernando Hierro

This hard-running midfield general plays a lead role in the Spanish side. His phenomenal work rate and stylish passing make him one of the most sought after players in European football.

However, despite his reputation as a top player, he disappointed many in Europe by failing to pot any of his glorious strikes – a lack of fitness seemed to be the main problem.

His venomous shot can leave keepers' gloves with a mark on them, making him a player who will always find a place in the national side and who will be remembered for a long time to come.

European Players

Flair, skill, passion are what the Portuguese try to incorporate in their game. At their best, they are probably on a par with the Brazilians but lack that bite which the boys from South America have.

In Euro 96, they dazzled with their marvellous skill and tricks, but failed to deliver that killer punch needed to win important matches. Players such as Rui Costa, Joao Pinto and Fernando Couto have so much talent yet cannot give Portugal the power and driving force they need. Portugal have come a long way in the past five years, when they never gave any team a decent fight and were regarded as 'nobodies' on the world scene; these days, with that extra push, they could be one of the most dangerous sides around.

Fernando Couto

The tall, well-built Portuguese centre back came to the European Championships to make his mark and to show the rest of Europe what he was capable of; and he certainly did this. With his soft touch but hard tackle, he had the strength which was otherwise lacking throughout the Portuguese team.

After the Championships, he generated major interest within the Premiership, attracting many top clubs, but no deals were done in the end and he decided to turn to the Spanish League instead.

Rui Costa

Before the Championships began, Portugal were considered the 'dark horses' of the competition, mainly due to their impressive midfield combination of Paulo Sousa and Rui Costa.

Rui Costa certainly lived up to expectations, displaying his world class skill and temperament on more that one occasion.

He was singled out, along with Sammer of Germany, as 'player of the tournament' and it was for this reason that big clubs like Arsenal were linked with a large transfer deal for the star.

Paulo Sousa

Paulo Sousa and Rui Costa are two of the brightest stars to come out of Portuguese football since Eusebio.

Sousa is a strong, hard-working midfielder who still likes to go forward and score goals, but Euro 96 proved to be quite a disappointment after so much had been promised by his standard of play for Juventus.

Sousa is now at the peak of his career and could very well help Portugal win trophies very soon.

European Players

Craig Brown and his side gave a sterling performance in Euro 96, giving great pleasure to their fans and putting Scotland back on the footballing map.

Their Euro 96 Championships began with a match against Holland; the resulting draw boosted the morale of the whole team. Players such as Colin Hendry and Gary McAllister showed that true grit and guts can reap rewards, although Gary McAllister would rather forget the long-awaited game against rivals, England; he missed a penalty which would almost certainly have earned Scotland a point.

Their final match will be remembered by every Scottish fan: with England beating the Dutch and Ally McCoist's wonder goal bringing Scotland victory over Switzerland, they needed one more goal, which they just could not find and so went out of the Championships with their heads held high.

Ally McCoist

Ally is a player who richly deserves the praise that he receives. A great ambassador for the game, he is now regarded as one of the best goalscorers in Scottish football history.

Unfortunately, over the years he has never really been able to translate his club form into country form; however, when finally given his chance in Euro 96, he rattled the net with one of the best goals of the tournament, and proved wrong all the critics who told him he was too old.

It seems that his international career may now be drawing to a close, but he is increasingly determined to play a major role in helping Rangers win another Scottish Championship trophy.

A team that came to Euro 96 with no reputation, no chance and no players? How wrong that was!

The Czech Republic had some jewels: Poborsky, Berger and Medved were top of the line but many others sparkled just at the right moment. Their first game against Germany, a 2-0 defeat, seemed to confirm everyone's initial expectations of both teams, but a rousing performance against Italy in the next game woke everyone up to a team that had players who were willing to work for each other and run all day long. The 2-1 win over Italy gave the Czechs a chance of qualification into the next stage; then a 3-3 draw against Russia – when their equalising goal was scored in the last minute – catapulted them into the quarter-finals. Karel Poborsky had impressed in every game, and his delightful lob eliminated Portugal sending the Czechs into the semis where they overcame the disappointing French on a penalty shoot-out.

In the final against Germany, they took and held the lead until the indefatigable Germans scored two goals in quick succession. However, the Czech Republic are potential giantkillers and mean business.

Patrik Berger

The handsome midfielder spent a large amount of his time in the Czech Republic modelling as well as playing football.

When he came to England during Euro 96, he proved to be a model professional, despite failing to be selected for the first game against Germany.

After his side's defeat, the manager realised that Berger must be included, and it was clear that the new addition to the line-up changed the team's performances drastically.

The Czech team progressed to the final, and it was Berger himself who scored their goal in the game against Germany, albeit from the penalty spot. His next job must be to guide the Czechs to France in 1998.

European Players

DENMARK

The Danes were unimpressive in Euro 96 and simply not up to the standard of four years ago when they won the trophy.

Brian Laudrup was the only real star of the tournament for Denmark. His twists, turns and vision brought life to an otherwise ordinary Denmark team. They were embarrassed by the Croatians, especially Davar Suker who showed up the great Peter Schmeichel like never before. Apart from an easy 3-0 win over a very poor Turkish side, they were terribly disappointing.

They need to bring in some new ideas and creativity if they are to succeed as they have done in the past.

Brian Laudrup

A tantalising forward player who seems to drift around the forward positions creating and putting away chances.

Denmark's chances in Euro 96 were limited, yet the ex AC Milan forward managed to sparkle in a very ordinary team.

His displays for Rangers and Denmark have caused him to be named as one of the most exciting players in Europe.

The Swiss came to the European Championships with very little hope, and therefore the pressure of getting results was not as intense as for the high-profile contenders.

They proved a major obstacle for Terry Venables' England team when they gave the home nation a tough game, drawing 1–1. Turkyilmaz was the major Swiss threat throughout the whole tournament – his strength and trickery gave defenders (especially Tony Adams) a run for their money. The Swiss then lost their next two games to Scotland and Holland with performances that lacked real passion and drive from the team. There was the plus point for the Swiss, that Vogel, a young midfielder, made his mark on the international scene with some very impressive performances.

The Swiss team should try and get their players to play to their full potential on a regular basis and as a collective whole. Players such as Chapuisat and Sforza are very talented, but need extra determination to produce their skills for their nation.

Kubilay Turkyilmaz

Since the loss of their manager Roy Hodgson, the Swiss camp has been in a state of confusion and discontent and it showed during the European Championships. There were no signs of the determined performances which took them into the final stages of the competition, and few signs of their talented stars.

If there was any consolation, it was Turkyilmaz's display in all three group matches.

His power and pace were a constant problem for all defenders, and it was no coincidence that he netted Switzerland's only goal of the Championship against England.

European Players

ROMANIA

A team with such quality and promise for the last four years proved that a club cannot survive without change, and the Romanians have kept the same players for so many years now, they are too old to compete with the cream of Europe.

Players like Popescu, Belodedici and Lacatus were found to be lacking pace and strength , and really held back any positive ideas that came out of the team. Hagi was very average for him, as was Raducioiu who scored Romania's only goal; these two really did not perform to their potential. They lost every game in Euro 96, but were very unlucky not to get a point when the impressive Munteanu scored a legitimate goal, which was disallowed.

The Romanian team can no longer rely on the players who initially brought them recognition; these players should serve as an example and inspiration to future teams.

Gheoghe Hagi

The super Romanian was dynamite in previous Championships and a real live-wire for his club last year, but could not come anywhere near that form for his country, even though they were relying heavily on his drive and enthusiasm to generate strength within the team – a team that looked old and lacked ideas. Hagi's talents, skills and influence must now be directed towards the coaching staff, and to training younger players up to his level of play.

After such a brilliant World Cup two years ago, Bulgaria were expected to give strong performances and maybe even challenge for a place in the final.

The team were disappointing; they looked old and there was little life in the squad. Hristo Stoichkov was the only player with any ideas and enough quality to play in these Championships. Players such as Penev, Balakov and Lechov were nowhere near their best and looked slow and unfit. Stoichkov ran the show, and his three goals saw them get four points in a competition where there were much better teams.

Much must be changed if the Bulgarians are to come anywhere near to recreating their performances of the World Cup 94. They must develop their youth side and bring some life into their squad, otherwise they will return to being the minnows of European football.

Hristo Stoichkov

Europe proved again that Hristo is the only real Bulgarian goal threat, and he is presumably getting tired of working the attacking strings of the team single-handedly, but to his credit he does the job superbly.

Having scored virtually all of Bulgaria's goals in the 1994 World Cup, he carried on to score all three of their goals in the Championships, and was once again the star player.

Hristo leads his country into the next World Cup qualifying campaign, but has very little team support and the Bulgarian team must inject some new talent if they are to reach anywhere near the height of two years ago.

European Players

European Players

The laid-back Croatians came into their first European Championships with a very good reputation and, after beating Italy in qualifying, they were feared by the other teams in their group.

With convincing wins over Turkey and Denmark they looked as though they had a chance of making a real name for themselves in the Championships. Yet their coach made a remarkable decision in the game against Portugal when all they needed was a point; he left out most of his best players and thus lost the game, which meant they had to play Germany in the quarter-finals. They gave the Germans a tough match but lacked focus and lost 2-1.

Players such as Bilic, Boban and Suker were simply outstanding and gave their country an extremely good name; this is what they came to Euro 96 to do.

Croatia are sure to carry on leading the red and white flag into major competitions where they'll play some breathtaking football.

Davar Suker

After such rave reviews for his club and country, Davar had a chance to show his talent to the world in Euro 96.

After a slow start to the tournament, he dazzled us with his amazing ability in the match against Denmark where he showed up a bewildered Peter Scheimechel with a superb goal and an audacious chip from the halfway line, which could be compared to a similar attempt by Pele.

Suker is now regarded as one of the hottest players in Europe and is one that we will see in many major competitions to come.

World Cup Preview 1998

With our nations building for the 1998 World Cup campaign, the next two years are sure to full of excitement and anticipation to see who will qualify.

Out of the five home nations, it seems that there is no sure group for anyone – with every team having at least one very difficult match. England are, of course, fully expected to qualify after a very impressive Euro 96; and with many young and exciting players like James, Campbell and Beckham surging into the first team squad, the future looks promising. Yet, with the Italians in the same group, England are not favourites and may have to settle for getting the best second runner-up place.

Ironically, Scotland appear to have a squad of less quality and depth, yet they seem to stand a better chance of getting first place; an unpredictable Swedish side and an ordinary Austrian team are what the Scottish face, and they are capable of overcoming both teams. Craig Brown has proved a positive manager with the strength of character to lead the Scottish flag to France in two years' time.

Mick McCarthy's Republic of Ireland side is going through many changes, and the pressure to recreate the form found under Jack Charlton is enormous. Possibly Mick lacks Jack's fighting qualities which is why the Republic will struggle to make an impact. With Romania in their group they can only be hoping for a runner-up spot, and are going to have to work hard for that.

Bobby Gould and Wales are starting to show promise, despite few resources. They may cause a few shocks, but the contrast in the team between experienced and inexperienced players is too big a divide and will halt their qualifying challenge. Northern Ireland and Bryan Hamilton are a hard-working side with a few players of world class talent, but the rest of the team consists of very average players who are more at home in the First Division than the world scene.

The ambition and capabilities of the Premiership teams make the World Cup qualifying campaign compelling, and lends a fresh approach to football. Glenn Hoddle sparks off a whole new era for England; he will be determined to lead his young lions into France to win the World Cup

Levinson Books would like to thank:
Kate Burns, Julie Chamberlain, Robert Cohen, Heather Ellis, Kristy Flowers, Warren Goldberg,
Marc Johnathan, James Lamb, Ben Lane, Louise Millar, Paul Oldman and Alan Stewart
for all their help in the production of this book.

Editor's Note:
The final date for compiling this book was October 1st 1996.
All reasonable efforts were made to ensure that the data was accurate at that time.
Player transfers and/or managerial changes after that date were, of course, beyond our control.